# LITTLE FARM IN THE GARDEN

## A PRACTICAL MINI-GUIDE TO RAISING SELECTED
## FRUITS AND VEGETABLES HOMESTEAD-STYLE

LITTLE FARM IN THE FOOTHILLS
BOOK THREE

SUSAN COLLEEN BROWNE

WHEGTHORN
PRESS

*Little Farm in the Garden: A Practical Mini-Guide to Raising Selected Fruits and Vegetables Homestead-Style*

Copyright © 2020 by Susan Colleen Browne

Ebook ISBN: 978-1-952470-00-4

Print ISBN: 978-1-952470-01-1

Published by Whitethorn Press

www.susancolleenbrowne.com

www.littlefarminthefoothills.blogspot.com

www.susancolleenbrowne.substack.com

Cover Photographs © John F. Browne

# ALSO BY SUSAN COLLEEN BROWNE

**Memoirs of Country Life**

*Little Farm in the Foothills: A Boomer Couple's Search for the Slow Life*

*Little Farm Homegrown: A Memoir of Food-Growing, Midlife and Self-Reliance on a Small Homestead*

**Irish Village of Ballydara Series**

*It Only Takes Once*

*Mother Love*

*The Hopeful Romantic*

*The Galway Girls*

*The Secret Well* (Short Story)

*The Christmas Visitor* (Short Story)

*The Little Irish Gift Shop*

*Becoming Emma*

*Becoming Emma Special Edition: With Two Fairy Cottage of Ballydara Short Stories*

*The Fairy Cottage of Ballydara*

**Middle Grade Fiction**

*Morgan Carey and The Curse of the Corpse Bride*

*Morgan Carey and The Mystery of the Christmas Fairies*

*The Secret Astoria Scavenger Hunt*

# WELCOME TO MY LITTLE FARM GARDEN

On this sunny spring morning, I gaze out at my garlic bed and the healthy, three-inch green tops poking out of the soil. It's a few days past the vernal equinox, and I'm seeing all the promise in this year's garden. The fall-planted garlic has sprouted, the wintered-over spinach is a rich green, and the leaves are almost big enough to harvest. Crinkly pinkish-green rhubarb leaves are just beginning to emerge, and the buds on the blueberry and caneberry plants are swelling. I look over the beds with fond satisfaction envisioning them full of healthy greenery, and eating the delicious fruits of our labor!

Surely food gardening is the ultimate in being optimistic. You put seeds in the ground and trust that most of them will germinate. Then you hover over your tiny seedlings, hoping for the most optimal weather so they'll grow and thrive. Then you wait patiently through the coming weeks or months, watching your crop throughout the growing season, looking forward to the day you can harvest.

A friend said the other day that she was a little blue, so she spent the afternoon in her garden, transplanted her new nursery plants, and her outlook brightened immediately. I always say there's nothing like raising food to create a feeling of deep contentment…not to mention a sense of independence.

And being more independent is why my husband John and I started our small homestead and got a lot more serious about producing our own food. As a food grower, I'm the author of true-life homesteading books—*Little Farm in the Foothills: A Boomer Couple's Search for the Slow Life* relates our first, tumultuous and eye-opening year on our country place. I share several more years of the ups and downs of our homesteading journey in the sequel, *Little Farm Homegrown: A Memoir of Food-Growing, Midlife, and Self-Reliance on a Small Homestead*. Given all the adventures and misadventures we've experienced since then, I'm already planning more Little Farm books for the future.

I teach a community college workshop as well, called "Grow a Homestead-Style Food Garden." I'm a Pollyanna kind of person, an eternal optimist—which I guess makes me a good candidate for gardening! Still, there are plenty of less-than-optimistic reasons to grow your own food. One of the first topics we discuss in class is that none of us knows what the future may bring; thus producing your own food supply can become a bulwark against uncertainty.

Yet when it comes to being forced to rely on the food we grow ourselves, our class discussions have always been theoretical: What if life changed, and the availability of our favorite foods became an issue?

Remember the Victory Gardens of the Second World War era? Food rationing meant you had to be creative about feeding yourself and your family. So folks who had the inclination and the space in their yard started a food garden. Now, the notion might seem kind of fun and quaint, but you never know…what if the foodstuffs we needed to be healthy and thriving (or even to sustain life) were no longer available to buy?

What if there were shifting weather patterns that could

impact local or national agricultural systems? Think of record-setting rains one year that drowned the Illinois pumpkin crop, or the Arctic blast in Texas that froze all the lettuce (along with the electrical grid).

Closer to home, our neighbor down the lane has raised beef cattle ever since we moved here. But because of changing temperatures and rainfall, his pasture is no longer productive enough to feed his herd. He's slowly selling it off, and is down to about one-quarter of the number of cattle he had before. (Happily, a few babies still show up every spring!)

We've all experienced storm-related power outages—on our place, we've had countless one to three-day outages. These brief outages aren't too hard to get through if you have a generator, and we have two of them: one for our house, to run an hour or two per day to keep the food in our fridge from spoiling, and a second generator for the pumphouse to power the well pump. But what about longer periods without electricity?

Some years back, my daughter who lives on the Oregon Coast experienced a one-hundred year windstorm and widespread regional power outages. Mud and rock slides had closed the two roads in and out of town. Without electricity, grocery stores were shuttered—and for one frightening week, she couldn't buy food for her young children. Luckily for her family, her in-laws lived seven miles away and had extra food on hand. But perhaps other families weren't so fortunate.

In my homestead-gardening class, we've also explored other potential difficulties. What if there are significant interruptions to our power grid, from cyber-terrorism or solar storms? That could mean power outages for many weeks. We could also be looking at alterations in food imports—items like tropical fruits or avocados or tomatoes in the dead of winter might be harder to come by...or no longer in stores.

What all these scenarios tell me is that you can't go wrong growing some of your own food. While raising some fresh nibbles to munch on is one of the great pleasures of food gardening, I believe producing fruits and vegetables that you depend on for food sources can be equally enjoyable! But it may take an entirely different mindset—and that's where this mini-guide comes in.

*Little Farm in the Garden* focuses on helping you grow food in what I call "homestead-style"—that is, raising fruits and vegetables without store-bought supplies, fertilizers and other gardening products. (Or using a minimum.) To me, homestead-style also means following sustainable and/or organic gardening methods whenever possible, and using what you have on hand.

The ultimate goal is to not only increase your self-reliance, but to live more simply and more locally. While I can't see John and me ever raising ALL our own food, we continue to move toward increasing our production and storage capabilities.

I will say that homestead-style gardening isn't for everyone. It can be fairly high- maintenance and may involve more intense physical labor—and if your priority is food-raising, beauty and aesthetics will definitely take a back seat! Yet whatever food-growing path you may take, my aim is to help you achieve your dream.

So, onward to the joys of food gardening!

# YOU CAN BEGIN WITH ONLY A DREAM

❧

*W*hen it comes to raising food, I'm not a proponent of 'Go Big or Go Home."

While beginning any project or goal, a wise friend of mine says, "Start where you are.' If you're short on food-growing space, you can find a lot of satisfaction in beginning with a pot of basil in your windowsill, or a container tomato plant on your deck. If you're committed to growing some food crops and have some gardening space in your yard, or a patch of grass you can tear out for beds, you can always start with that. My friend is also fond of saying, "there is no rush." You can learn as you go, and expand your garden over time. As my dear father-in-law used to tell us, "You can't eat an elephant in one bite."

Before we left the city for the country life, my husband John and I had a small "kitchen garden" in our yard. Four raised veggie beds, a half-dozen blueberry bushes, a few raspberry plants, a monster boysenberry, plus six fruit trees— all of which supplemented (in a very modest way) the food we bought at the grocery store.

When we came up with a dream to sell our city home and buy some acreage, that vision was based on our desire for space and quiet, as much for the opportunity to expand our food growing. Once we did sell our house and move, our dream, our creativity and our energy expanded too.

Our little homestead/backyard farm is 10 acres of a former clearcut in the Foothills of the Cascade Mountains. Our acreage is up on a ridge and covered with multiple species of native blackberries, so we came up with the name, "Berryridge Farm."

Fourteen years ago this spring, John and I started with bare ground and hand tools. Over the years, we've built a relatively small but productive food-growing setup that keeps us in organic fruits and vegetables year round. As for self-reliance, John and I aren't interested in hoarding food in a secret bunker or anything—which in these difficult days, doesn't exactly sound like a bad idea. Still, even if you amassed a year's worth of food or more, it would eventually run out. If you stored more food supplies than that, you'd have to devise a strategy to use up, then replenish your supply, or do both concurrently—and that could start to get really complicated.

However, with a homestead-style garden, you'll have food you can count on year after year after year. For John and me, our goal started as a way to create our own homegrown food supply, and to reduce our dependence on grocery items.

When it comes to creating or expanding your garden, your dream can also depend on how many helpers you have! I am blessed to have John as a homesteading partner. He's brought a range of expertise to our place: he was growing food in a small yard long before I met him. John's been a contributor to both my books, and on our place, he's in charge of infrastructure. We had a contractor build a 1700-square foot pole building for a barn/shop, but John has constructed all our wood sheds and storage sheds, in addition to our fences and raised beds. He also does the tree felling for firewood and most of the wood processing, and keeps the woodstove burning eight months of the year.

While we're pretty relaxed with our respective job descriptions—he helps with transplanting, and I lend a hand with wood chopping—I generally run the food-growing side of our little homestead: planting, weeding, watering, harvesting, and putting up. If you have kids to help, or other interested family members or neighbors, why not partner up and enlist their time and energy? Everyone benefits! And you can all learn from each other.

In my "Homestead-Style" workshop I mentioned previously, my students and I have shared resources, experiences, and tips, which has enhanced my own food gardening. At our place, raising our fruits and vegetables has been a steep learning curve at times, but through my 20+ years of food gardening, taking workshops, keeping a detailed garden journal and lots of other research, I've figured out what works and how to raise a range of crops for a successful harvest in our climate and in similar ones: specifically, mild, short-season climates like the maritime Pacific Northwest, USA.

I've also learned a lot of what **not** to do! I have related our many errors and missteps in my two memoirs, and this booklet won't be any different. My feeling is, by sharing what John and I have done wrong, I can help *you* avoid the same mistakes.

This guide will be most useful for the relatively **cool, moist climate on the west side of the Cascade Mountains**. Our own Foothills microclimate has its own quirks. Our acreage sits in a valley between two foothills, so there's a kind of cold sink in our immediate area. In the winters, it can snow at our place, yet rain one mile down the main road.

On the other hand, we've created our food garden on the south side of our house and barn/shop, so it's kind of like a heat island. Also, while our region is considered maritime, our larger Foothills area is about 35 miles from the bays and inlets leading to the Pacific Ocean. With that distance, and a higher elevation, we have hotter summers and colder, snowier winters than parts of our county closer to the water.

The Foothills also receives more precipitation than areas south and west of us. From Berryridge Farm, our view to the east is a massive foothill of over 5,000 feet, which as the crow flies, is about two-thirds of a mile away. As the clouds bring moisture in from the west, they'll pile up against that foothill and then comes the rain.

If you garden in a different kind of climate, my hope is that this booklet can still be useful, in terms of general guidelines for cultivation. You can always adjust your seed-planting, maintenance and harvesting timetable according to a large variety of factors: your area's rainfall, temperature ranges, first and last frost dates for your area, your soil type, and any other factors that may apply.

**And please keep in mind: Like any other kind of advice, suggestions or recommendations, whether they're about gardening, auto repair, or managing your finances, take what's in this mini-guide with a grain of salt! What works for John and me in our garden might not work for you, so use what you think might be helpful and let go of anything else.**

My ultimate aim for this booklet is to present **a big picture of creating your own reliable food system**—and hopefully help you approach growing food with confidence and produce a bounty of fruits and vegetables!

# EVOLUTION OF A HOMESTEAD GARDEN

❧

*W*hile our story of starting a food garden will be different from yours and everyone else's, the steps John and I took to create ours can illustrate that there's no such thing as an instantly productive garden setup. It can take many months, and for year-round production, even many seasons to get up to speed. Yet, as I said before, I hope you can learn from what we did, especially the mistakes we made! I've posted a few photos of our food garden on my website and I'll be adding more.

**OUR FIRST SEASON in the Foothills:**

John and I moved into our country place in the midst of a rainy April. Our 1300 square-foot house sat on a cleared ½-acre patch of rocky ground, with a bleak view of bare, compacted soil, thanks to the bulldozer s work. Not exactly an auspicious beginning.

For one thing, compacted soil contains very little air, when you need lots of air between soil particles (25%!) for cultivating crops. Additionally, all this earth-moving during a record-setting winter rain had been very damaging to the soil—fertile soil has a "structure" so disturbing all those particles, microbes, and mineral molecules can impact your food production.

Also, all the rocks and gravel (our county sits on huge deposits of gravel) in our future garden meant there wasn't much fertility left in the yard—the bulldozer had basically scraped off the topsoil. That topsoil mostly ended up in the piles of stumps and wood slash our site developer shoved to the edges of the ½ acre. Sadly, that soil was basically unrecoverable.

In terms of homesteading prospects, there was good news and bad news. The good news was that our place had super drainage for an on-site septic system—bad news, it would take time to both build up our soil for food gardening and let nature rebound. John and I didn't see an earthworm in the garden for about three years. Still, we had a few small patches of fertile ground in the yard: from the clear-cut forest, there was some build-up of leaf mold and decomposing wood, and our garden site had never been cultivated. So some of the elements and compounds that aid in fertility could still be in the soil.

As I mentioned previously, homestead-style gardening means utilizing what you have on hand. We learned that while our country place in the Foothills was only forty miles from our former city home, the climate here is quite different: far cooler nights, and a considerably shorter growing season. So we needed warmth for our garden.

And we had LOTS of rocks to work with. Solution: as we developed garden areas in our rocky, gravel-filled site, unearthing piles and piles of rocks, we surrounded our future garden beds with the largest stones to warm the soil. The ground was way too rocky for a Rototiller, so we busted up our garden spaces with a pick-ax. Which meant we carved out areas for beds very slowly, one at a time.

Also, in the spirit of using what you have on hand, our

clearcut was surrounded by acres of birch and alder saplings. We saved a lot of money using them for fence posts!

In the midst of all this labor, I longed for a bit of civilization. I leveled a small area next to the house and laid patio bricks for a spot to put a lawn chair—not that I had much time for sitting! Next on my list was a bed for a pollinator garden...useful for far more than looking pretty. (We'll go into more detail about pollinating plants later.)

That first summer, as we created garden beds, eager to start planting, we faced one major roadblock that every food gardener must confront: **One of your 1st considerations for food self-reliance is providing protection from wildlife.** Back in our former city, which has a lot of greenbelts, deer are EVERYWHERE. They have completely overrun every neighborhood, and have devoured many a city-dweller's garden.

Here in the Foothills, the deer were no different, and we found that without proper fencing, we would put every single nursery plant at risk. While our garden beds seemed safe enough with sapling fence posts and casually-strung steer wire, we couldn't depend on this jerry-rigged approach for our permanent crops. So our next move was to build a sturdy, permanent deer fence for our orchard.

It seems funny now, but at the time, we thought of deer as Public Enemy #1. They cost us a great deal of time, labor, and money for fencing. Little did we know what other pests could do to your food growing!

One of our first shopping trips was to Lowe's to buy fence posts and wire. John and I figured, while we're here, let's buy our veggie starts. We put the little plants into the ground right away, but they didn't really grow for about six weeks. We then looked at the tags and discovered the starts were from a nursery in Alabama. It was our first lesson in going local: buy your nursery starts from a climate similar to your garden. We moved toward starts grown in the Pacific NW, then grown in our county.

By August, I had installed a flowerbed (a happy coincidence that the space was one of those patches of fertile ground) to bring in bees and other pollinators. Although we'd raised only a token amount of food, **John and I were certain we were off to a great start!**

Can you see the "but..." coming? The rest of that first year on our homestead was a series of mistakes, misadventures and out-and-out hardships, which I relate in my first memoir, *Little Farm in the Foothills.* Our real troubles began six months after moving in, in October: our well went dry and had to be re-drilled, we experienced two major power outages and had no generator, our water system froze, and our lane was completely blocked by snow. When the road had become barely passable, we had a medical emergency. To top it off, we were using a woodstove to heat the house, but we had almost no dry firewood.

On some level, John and I were pretty traumatized with those three months of misfortune. After eight months at our new place we had to wonder, had we done the right thing, moving here? But we'd fallen in love with the homesteading lifestyle. And seeing no way we could ever again live in a city, there was no going back.

## Second Season:

Our second year in the Foothills, we embarked on building more infrastructure.

As John started constructing a new fence to surround our entire ½ acre, I expanded our gardening beds for more food growing. That meant pick-axing and hand-tilling with a spading fork through more rough, rocky ground. Two reasons for digging by hand: first, to preserve the soil structure, and second: we couldn't afford to go into debt for a tractor. However, I did enlist John for the biggest digging job: the one-foot deep trench for asparagus.

Protecting our crops became front-and-center. Although we had a sturdy deer fence surrounding our food-growing areas, rabbits found their way through the tiniest gaps. With rabbit predation, we discovered they'll devour just about any food crop. If there's a chance rabbits are around your home, consider surrounding all your food crops with one-inch poultry wire. Rabbits don't bother potatoes, tomatoes, hardy herbs, or pretty much all squash varieties, but for everything else, it's open season! They have nibbled my new garlic sprouts in the winter and early spring. To my chagrin, I discovered bunnies will even eat flowers, particularly soft annuals like pansies, lobelia, and nasturtiums, so protect those too.

By summer, my treasured perennial bed had more than fulfilled the old saying about perennials: "first year they sleep, the second year they creep, the third year they leap." In one year, the plants had moved right into the leap stage! August brought significant garden bounty: we had installed a strawberry bed, and we were harvesting zucchinis, brussel sprouts, winter squash, potatoes, and still picking late peas. John and I had a new confidence that everything was coming together!

Note: you can plant your veggies in any pattern you like, but I found it easier to get around with rows. It's a good idea to avoid walking on your beds because that creates soil compaction. John likes a polished look, so he created gravel pathways throughout the garden areas. A clean, organized look might not last for long, though, since weeds will eventually grow in gravel too!

THIRD SEASON:

Over the winter, John and I both devoured the food-growing memoir by Barbara Kingsolver, *Animal, Vegetable, Miracle,* and gotten even more inspired to raise our game. We decided that we wanted to not only supplement our food supply, but grow as much of our own food as we could. We could increase our self-sufficiency with bigger harvests, and store food for winter. Thus, we began further garden expansion: two more trenches for asparagus, making 33 crowns total.

As I began creating beds all the way to the edge of our original cleared ground, John and I were getting more knowledgeable about raising food in short-season climate. Garlic became a mainstay crop, and we discovered one of the joys of early spring in the Foothills is the garlic tips showing!

With greater self-reliance in mind, John planted two walnut trees. While our diet had plenty of fruits and veggies, now we would have a homegrown protein source! Still, the nursery staff gave us fair warning: "you don't plant walnuts for yourselves, you plant them for your grandkids." A walnut tree can take 30 years to produce a full crop. A couple of years ago, we harvested six nuts—and a year later, we had eleven. One homestead-style tool that comes in handy is patience!

After planting the walnut trees at the edge of our garden (oh, the mistakes we made!), we discovered walnut leaves exude a sort of toxic substance. Food crops won't grow near them. John ended up transplanting the trees to a woodsy area, and luckily deer haven't shown the least interest. That same year, I installed a second pollinator bed, and our orchard trees had a growth spurt. We had ended up with our first truly amazing harvest, and what felt like a stupendous amount of crops to store for winter: 60 pounds of potatoes, dozens of onions and 15 giant blue Hubbard squashes.

We didn't—and still don't—have a root cellar, since there are so many rodents around here it would have to be a concrete bunker-style structure. Still, we had plenty of room in the shop for storage.

Here comes another "little did we know" event: One month after tucking the potato crop into the shop for storage, we had a record snowfall, four feet of snow in about two weeks. I realize that's nothing compared with what a lot of folks get, but when you live on a private lane with no snowplowing service, that much snow is a real inconvenience. The real kicker, however, was the northeaster wind that accompanied the snow, bringing single-digit temperatures and numerous power outages.

Too late, I remembered all those potatoes and onions and squashes I'd stored in the un-insulated shop. They were all frozen solid: an entire winter's worth of spuds, and those beautiful Blue Hubbards would have kept us in side dishes and pies until spring. I felt very sad and bleak and yes, stupid as I threw them away. What I learned: bring storage crops indoors during major freezes. True, it's a hassle to haul in your crops, but as the saying goes, when needs must.

FOURTH SEASON:

**While last year we'd raised our game, this year brought a big shift in consciousness.**

I had read *Animal, Vegetable, Miracle* a couple more times over the last year, and John and I got inspired to move toward sustainable food growing. That meant moving away from a more conventional food supply and buying food from local sources when possible. Also we began phasing out buying nursery starts, and growing more crops from seeds.

John and I embarked on creating significantly more ground for food-raising, beyond the original ½ acre. By hand, we cleared two large spaces of trees and brush for more garden/orchard space. The total came to about 4,000 square feet. As in years past, we didn't seriously consider hiring out the job. The cost was still a big consideration.

Yet as John and I grew aware of all the small wildlife that

enhances your food garden—beneficial bugs, native bees and other pollinators, frogs and toads, birds, earthworms and garter snakes, etc.—running an excavator or bulldozer would not only disturb the soil but cause widespread destruction of wildlife and their habitat. Once the ground was cleared, we used materials we had on hand—in this case, creating raised veggie beds with logging slash—instead of building a retaining wall with purchased materials.

For the first time, I planted **organic** seed potatoes—they weren't yet available locally, but I was able to source them from our neighboring county. I had learned that **conventional potatoes** are raised with lots of pesticides and fungicides: they're on the "dirty dozen" list of produce. I had also read about a commercial potato grower in our state who didn't want his family eating their farm's own conventionally raised crop, so he had planted an organic potato patch in their food garden. So, organic seemed like the wise choice.

We had our first rhubarb harvest—like many "permaculture" food crops, it takes several years (three is fairly standard for a lot of permanent plants) for a rhubarb crown to produce a crop. From author Barbara Kingsolver, I got the epiphany (well, it was a new idea to me), that rhubarb was not only for dessert!

Part of my journey toward local food began the day I read the label of the Minute Mail orange juice I was drinking. Turns out, it was made out of juice concentrate from Brazil! It was the last can of Minute Maid I ever bought. I vowed from then on to eat fruit in season if possible, or homegrown frozen, and I began cooking stewed rhubarb for breakfast.

On the subject of rhubarb, keep in mind there's a certain technique for harvesting. You don't use a knife to cut it at the soil level; instead, you grasp the stalk at the base and pull gently, until the white, bottom portion of the stalk separates from the crown. This helps preserve the structure of the crown so it can continue to produce more leaves and stalks!

I had soon learned that the relaxed sort of netting we used around our city strawberry patch was completely inadequate for country pests. Nets had to be tightly installed! We had a fabulous strawberry crop, and John and I ate strawberries twice a day, a dish for breakfast and on shortcake for dinner dessert. After sharing berries with family and friends, we still had 20 quarts to freeze for winter.

We had a warm summer, which meant a bountiful tomato and winter squash crop. Our onion, asparagus, and bean crop was lush too. **However, this season turned out to be our last year of great production with crops planted in the ground.** (More on that later too.)

**FIFTH SEASON:**

We embarked on our most ambitious project to date: My birthday gift to John was six pullets we purchased from a home-steading family about 25 miles away. Once we increased our self-sufficiency with raising laying hens, we were able to share eggs with our family, plus we had a couple of paying customers too!

When it came to our flock of hens, John and I had another significant learning curve. We didn't have a conventional pasture for our "girls," but gave them LOTS of ground to roam around in, with abundant greens and other weeds. I'd been quite inspired by a magazine photo I'd seen, with chickens pecking around someone's lovely backyard, very picturesque. Then just weeks after we'd brought the chickens home, we discovered the real story: Hens can devastate any area you let them in!

One of our girls' roaming areas was one of the orchards, about a 40 x40 space. In less than a month, they'd scratched up every shoot, bug, every living thing. So upon our discovery that hens need far more pasture space than we'd ever dreamed, we doubly regretted having only ½ acre cleared. The hens could've used at least a ¼ acre alone just for free-ranging.

We'd continued to transplant more native plants from the woods closer to our food-growing areas. Our favorite native is one of the first spring blossoming plants around: red currant. By bringing in early flowering plants, long before the last frost of the season, you can encourage native pollinators, and be all set for your food crops' blossom time.

We began to see some significant food production kick in for our permanent plantings, like blueberries. I attribute much of that abundance to having a super-healthy population of native pollinating insects in the yard.

This was also the season we'd begun to move from simply starting crops to more long-term maintenance. For example: to keep our strawberry supply going, we created a new strawberry bed. Strawberry plants "wear out" after just a few seasons, succumbing to unpreventable viruses. My gardening books say the plants will bear three-five years, but in our garden, it seems they last three years tops. Since then, we've planted at least one bed with new strawberry crowns every other year.

I decided to try something really new: my big grain experiment. In terms of creating a homegrown balanced food supply, we had fruits and veggie and protein from our hens' eggs. So now we needed grains for complex carbohydrates! I'd read that barley is easy to thresh, so a barley crop would mean grains/scratch for the hens and John and I would have whole grains for cereal. Happily, I found an organic seed company from the neighboring county, with locally-raised grains. (But expensive: One packet of about 25 seeds = $4.)

By this time in our homesteading journey, costs took a back seat to moving forward, so I bought the seeds. Then I made one of my more spectacular miscalculations: pressed for open garden space, I planted the barley seeds along the edge of our strawberry beds. And discovered, too late, that every crop really needs its own dedicated bed.

I really hadn't thought this through: just because a slender stalk of grain can fit into a narrow slot, doesn't mean you should plant your seeds there. Adding insult to injury, the stalks got tangled up in the berry nets. Lesson: to give each crop the opportunity to succeed, allow plenty of room both between plants and between crops. That way, you'll have more water and more nutrients available for everything you grow. If there are nets involved, keeping crops separate means it's far easier and more convenient to effectively manage your garden spaces.

That summer, John and I were scratching our heads over a mystery taking place in our garden. Throughout the yard, the veggie plants seemed less vigorous, and our harvests were far smaller than the previous year. And there was one clue that had us both completely stumped. All of our large potatoes had big bites in them; many smaller potatoes had chunks missing too. Onion roots were stunted, and numerous vegetable seedlings were disappearing, almost before our very eyes. It took some research, but we discovered the culprit: VOLES.

Not moles. Moles eat bugs, and as you know, leave unsightly piles of dirt in your yard. If only that was our problem!

I'd never heard of voles before, but now, with my own eyes I saw confirmation of my research: that voles can cause more destruction in the home garden than just about any other critter. You see, voles are vegetarians that live in tunnels below the surface of the soil. Safe underground, they'll eat root crops, including the aforementioned potatoes, as well as carrots and parsnips. As I discovered in my broccoli and beet beds, they will pull a seedling from below, leaving only a hole. And you'll love this: sitting in a little hole, voles will munch on any strawberries resting on the ground, occasionally dashing from their hideaway to raid your berries wholesale.

John and I had to do something drastic, or else our homestead dream would vanish into dust.

**The remedy was to protect the crops from the ground up, in raised, screened beds.**

We had to basically retool our entire food-growing operation, one bed at a time. John constructed raised box garden beds, using lumber for the sides and ½ inch hardware cloth mesh on the bottom. He used non-treated fir, since wood preservatives in treated lumber will leach into your soil and your crops. Over time, we've replaced most of our garden space with boxed beds.

It sounds like a win-win, but it wasn't. First there's the cost. Between purchasing the lumber and a roll of hardware cloth ($100-$150), the total per box came to about $40. Then there's the labor: it took John several hours per box to hammer the sides together and cut and staple the mesh to the bottom.

Another challenge with boxed beds is the backbreaking job of moving all the dirt! You must severely disturb the soil, first digging out an area to set the bed in, then piling the soil back in. I found that the first year of a crop in a new boxed bed wasn't very productive. I had to rebuild the soil in the bed, using compost and/or organic material like leaves.

The other drawback was that being forced to utilize raised beds, John and I no longer had unlimited room for food-growing. We had to dial back our dreams of producing an ever-expanding homegrown food supply.

Remember that raised bed we made with logging slash? Without protection from below, every vegetable we planted in that spot was a wash. The potatoes were a failure, so we planted corn, and got only a few stunted plants for our troubles. Finally, John and I planted a 2nd blueberry patch. The voles have hit the blueberry roots as well, but the bushes have survived—and thrived. We had a couple of other blueberry bushes near our vegetable beds that were nearly destroyed by voles, but after we transplanted them inside a mesh cage, they have bounced back.

SUMMING UP:

As you see, our first five years of homesteading were definitely a boom-and-bust experience. Since then, John and I have carried on through more garden and life challenges, more ups and downs. Still, I hope this history will give you some ideas about what to expect when you're developing your own food garden, and the roadblocks you may encounter.

I'll also add that many of the mistakes we made were painful, both financially and to our homesteading ambitions and spirits! But we have learned from each one, which has given us not only patience with the process, but acceptance with the way Mother Nature *always* prevails.

# HOMESTEAD FOOD-RAISING: BASIC NUTS AND BOLTS

~~~
✦
~~~

*I*'ve found it's helpful to build your homestead-style food garden in steps. Consider creating: 1) Infrastructure, like fences and supports, 2) Orchard trees and other permanent plants, 3) Pollinating plants, and finally, 4) Annual crops.

I mentioned infrastructure like deer fencing and rabbit protection in the previous chapter; John has also built trellises for the cane berries. It's much harder to install fencing and supports after you've planted something, so you'll save time and energy and a whole lot of hair-pulling by getting your infrastructure in first.

### PERMANENT PLANTINGS in the Homestead Garden

Although orchard trees and other permanent plants may take several years to produce a crop, I like to think of them as food insurance. The weather could impact your veggie yields: in a cool, rainy summer, your seeds could rot in the ground. Or seedlings could wilt during unusual hot spells. What if you have a power outage? If you're dependent on a well, with no power, you won't have water for your annual vegetables. With permanent plants, however, you may still produce something to eat.

So for food self-reliance, to feed yourselves and your family, consider planting more than 1-season vegetables, and install plants that will feed you year after year. Permanent plants are the gift that keeps on giving. Here are some approximate time-frames for some common home garden permanent plants:

Rhubarb and asparagus, 15 years +

Berries: strawberries, 3-5 years, cane berries like raspberry, boysenberry, marrionberry, up to 15 years, blueberries, up to 50!

Fruit trees, if well managed, could bear for decades.

Perennial herbs, especially hardier types like oregano, sage, rosemary, and thyme, will keep chugging along year after year too.

When we started out, although we made that error with the Alabama-grown veggie starts, we purchased permanent plants from a local nursery with a similar climate, which grows their stock semi-sustainably. These starts—berries, fruit trees, and asparagus crowns—were more expensive than at the big box nurseries, but they were much higher quality. For optimal results, aim to get your permanent nursery plants into the ground in fall or early spring, and try not to let them sit in the pots too long before planting!

If John and I had a chance for a do-over, we would have planted all our blueberries/cane berries, rhubarb and asparagus in raised, screened beds. In the asparagus bed alone, voles have heavily impacted growth and production; about a third of the crowns we planted simply disappeared.

Caring for your permanent plants can include protecting the truck of young orchard trees: plant them inside those little blue tubes, since mice will eat the bark at the soil line and decimate the more tender roots. Also, around young trees, try to keep grass to a minimum. Grass creates lots of competition, sucking up water and nutrients you'd rather direct toward your tree.

John and I started with around 25 fruit trees, mostly apple trees, for our orchard plantings. However, we made the mistake of selecting lots of trees that we WANTED to grow, not trees that would thrive in our cool, damp climate.

One of our first experiments was a fig tree! Why? This variety had seemed healthy at the nursery, and we thought a fig would be cool. Reality: our fig died in the first winter northeaster. Another error: we planted two apricot trees, although the Frost peach back in our city garden had been rife with blight and fungus. Sure enough, with each season, more and more twigs and branches of the apricot trees turned black from fireblight. We were doing that Pollyanna thing, being overly optimistic—wanting to believe apricot trees would survive in the even cooler and wetter weather of the Foothills.

We also installed several varieties of heirloom and other apple varieties without any fungal or blight resistance, simply because we wanted them, like Ashmead's Kernel.

John, being a lover of pears and stone fruits, planted two pear trees and five plum. The pears produced nothing but spotted leaves and not a sign of fruit. While the European "prune" plums have survived, the Japanese varieties proved to be too susceptible to blight and other fungal diseases like black spot and black knot.

As blight and funguses impacted the vulnerable trees more each year, the situation was clear: these trees would never, ever thrive, and never produce a decent crop. Over time, we took out three plum trees, the two apricots, both pears and two heirloom apple trees. It was an expensive mistake: $250-$300 worth of nursery stock.

I found that the best way to save time, money, and energy is to grow what is suited for your area and the growing conditions of your garden.

. . .

### Siting Your Garden and Microclimates

To give your homestead garden the best chance of success, consider it as a food system that works as a unified whole. Permanent plants tend to be a little more forgiving and more resilient when it comes to many factors: water, sunlight, and the need for fertilizer; competition from other plants or weed pressure; and inconsistent or unseasonable temperatures.

Annual vegetables are the fussy, delicate members of the plant spectrum—and for them, you may want to be more strategic. I suggest that your first consideration should be making sure you're planting in a suitable growing space! In the cool, maritime climate of our homestead, sun and warmth for a vegetable garden is a priority. As I mentioned previously, now that we were growing food in the Foothills, with much cooler summer nights than our city garden, we looked for spots that would be warm and get lots of light—generally south-facing.

Most food crops need full sun, and 6-8 hours of sun is optimal; veggies like greens do tolerate part sun. Keep in mind if you see a plant label that says full sun or part sun, that will mean **morning sun**. Lettuce, cucumbers, maybe zucchinis, carrots too, can still thrive with a little shade in the later afternoon. Our first year, we made the mistake of planting vegetables against the west side of the house, since we figured it would be warm. The problem: that side of the house had no sunshine until one or two in the afternoon. The plants basically just sat there all summer and didn't produce anything.

Also, try not to plant vegetables close to trees: not just fir trees, but also fruit trees, even young ones. I learned that planting areas near trees are basically unproductive for veggies, kind of like a desert. In our earlier years (again, that Pollyanna thing), I planted vegetables in what I call "pocket plots" in our orchards. What I learned was this mantra: "Your garden is your garden, your orchard is your orchard."

The result of growing veggies in the orchard: stunted plants that didn't produce squat. Upon inspecting the little plots more closely, I found the soil was pale, dry and crumbly, even soon after rain. Another lesson: trees being the bigger plant, with a very large root system, will absorb the available water and nutrients in the areas surrounding them, leaving none for your small plants.

**GETTING STARTED with Planting and Cultivation:**

Many of you might not have a big swathe of bare soil for your garden beds. One idea is to convert some lawn areas, or any sunny space that's weedy or otherwise not earning its keep. To convert these spaces is an easy (if time-consuming) two-step process. In the **fall**, lay cardboard or newspaper on the grass or weeds as a "killing" mulch. Then cover the cardboard with yard clippings, wood chips or whatever you'd got on hand to completely block the light. By spring, pull up the mulch and cardboard and you'll find fertile soil with lots of earthworms.

A tip I will mention again: try not to walk on your beds, either existing or future ones, as this destroys the air pockets in the soil. If you must walk in your beds, lay down boards or planks and step on those.

By now you might have ideas for your permanent food plants and spaces for your garden beds…what to plant next?

Many of your crops will have flowers that need pollination: fruit trees, berries, squash, tomatoes, peas, and so forth. Developing a healthy and diverse little garden ecosystem will enhance your chances of a successful harvest. This system ideally includes pollinator-friendly plantings for attracting birds, bees and butterflies, and other insects (including good bugs that might eat the bad bugs), and other beneficial wildlife. One helpful approach is to select a variety of plants that suits your yard and growing spaces, adding native plantings in **appropriate locations** to provide a balanced environment.

Let's picture a field of a conventional farm, say, corn or wheat: it's a monoculture, with many acres of one crop planted in rows. For optimum yields, there are no other types of plants to compete with the crop. These conventional crops require lots of fertilizer and herbicides. In our area, raspberries are a common monoculture. A one-crop system is efficient, and produces lots of food you can harvest with machines.

We home food gardeners can do things differently, and include both food crops and other beneficial plants in our yard. However, I recommend that you don't necessarily install those non-food crops in the same bed. As I mentioned, veggies need a great deal coddling in terms of light, water and nutrients.

## Working with Nature

If you have space, native plants can enhance your small garden ecosystem, provided you don't plant them right next to your crops. Natives are generally drought-tolerant, low maintenance and help support a range of beneficial species. Here at Berryridge Farm, we're surrounded by natives in the forest understory: Indian plum, red currant, honeysuckle, native filbert, thimbleberry and salmonberry, and wildflowers like daisies, fireweed and foxglove, all of which attract pollinators.

In the yard, we transplanted red currant, native bleeding heart, and swordfern. Besides the native trees surrounding us, we have salal and Oregon grape—all those natives provide food and shelter not only for pollinators, but for birds, and the "good garden friends" (as John says) that I mentioned previously, like ladybugs, frogs and toads.

Let me emphasize, however, that any natives you plant in your garden will grow far better than they do in the wild! So site them carefully. And the more space and light you give them, the more prolifically they grow. We made the mistake of transplanting Oregon grape into the yard instead of leaving it in the woods. Then discovered that it grows like a carpet with roots of steel! (And please don't get me started about the swordfern we brought in. Ferns have massive root systems and tearing them out takes far more energy than I'd ever guessed.)

As I mentioned in Chapter 2, shortly after we moved in I installed flowering perennials from the nursery to attract pollinators, for the long-term benefits to our food garden. Pollinators are essential, and definitely the more the merrier!

Consider the almond orchards in California—these orchards are another monoculture, where growers must bring in honeybees to pollinate the trees. Travel is extremely hard and stressful for the bees, and many thousands die. Happily for home gardeners, if we want pollinators for our flowering crops, we can do things differently.

**Natives + cultivated plants = a balanced garden!** All kinds of pollinators will be attracted to a diverse garden containing lots of different types of plants. Mason bees are native bees, and one of the most efficient pollinators since they don't make honey! (Honeybees use lots of energy bringing pollen to their hives for honey-making.) More native pollinators include bumblebees, smaller bees, butterflies, beneficial wasps, small flying insects, even houseflies and ants pollinate, plus hummingbirds! With a pollinator-friendly garden, you have best chance of high production in your food garden.

Since a lot of cultivated flowers don't bloom until midsummer, you can get a head start by bringing early-blossoming plants into your food garden; early flowers will attract pollinators long before you plant vegetables. Native flowers like red currant and bleeding heart bloom here in early April, and your orchard blossoms will attract lot of pollinators too.

Cultivated varieties that attract bees and other pollinators, and are easy to grow:

*Daffodils/narcissus for early pollinators like bumblebees and mason bees. We've seen bees sleeping inside the blossoms on chilly days!

*Violas (the small pansy varieties): At our place, they grow as easily as native plants, re-seeding and spreading prolifically, and can bloom from early spring until frost. Bunnies will eat them down to the quick, so give them some protection!

*Coneflowers, often called Echinacea

*Crocosmia

*Bee balm

*Hardy herbs like sage, oregano, mints, thyme and lavender

*Coral bells/Heuchera/Purple Palace: the purple-leaved varieties can have white or pink blossoms

Something extra to consider regarding pollinator-friendly plantings, especially flower varieties that attract hummingbirds: take care installing them near any fruits and veggies you're protecting with poultry wire. I avoid planting red current, bee balm, and coral bells too close to where I've got poultry fencing—hummingbirds buzz around at such high speeds that perhaps even with their adept navigation, they might not always see the fencing in time. John and I once found a dead hummingbird lodged tight inside the wire's one-inch weaving. We figured, sadly, that it got stuck in the small space and died of fright. Caring for wildlife often means keeping the big picture of your garden in mind!

Some flower species are helpful for pollinators but can be problematic. Examples:

Black-eyed Susan: They both reseed readily and send out runners—they have turned up all over our yard. Weeding them is a pain, as the roots are some of the toughest I've encountered! However, little birds like chickadees and sparrows love to eat the seeds during fall and winter.

A friend gave me a couple of pots of what she called Bachelor's buttons: a broad-leaf perennial with a delicate filigree of blue blossoms. Handing over the pots, she said merrily, "you can't kill 'em." I was all for resilient plants, and I'd heard bees liked blue flowers, so into the garden they went. I've regretted it ever since. It's the most invasive perennial ever, and if that's not bad enough, it attracts ants. Turns out, ants love decomposing wood, and surrounded as we are by nine acres of clearcut logging slash, we already have huge populations of ants. And when it comes to these plants, YOU REALLY CAN'T KILL THEM. I've dug out their roots, tried to smother them, covered them with boulders, buried them under weed piles; still, they live on.

**Other Ways to Work with Nature**

Part of homestead-style food gardening is getting accustomed to less-than-beautiful produce. All those fruits and veggies in the grocery store, even the organic varieties, are grown with an array of pesticides, herbicides, fungicides, fertilizers and soil amendments that might not be available to you. Or many of them would be very high maintenance to use.

For example, we grow Florina apples using no sprays or fungicide. They ripen late, after the fall rains have begun. By the time you pick them at the end of October, the fruit is covered with faint dark spots: fungus. It's harmless, and when you wash the apples you can rub off the spots.

John and I spoke to a conventional apple grower in our county who told us you can't grow organic apples commercially in our damp, cool climate; there are just too many funguses. Many of the apples we grow are prone to scab; they aren't particularly pretty, but they're fine for cooking. If eating fresh, you can cut away any spots.

However, a lot of scab on your apples probably means the tree is not well-suited for raising without spraying; the yield may continue to shrink as well. John and I have a Tsugaru apple whose fruit is very scabby. After getting nothing but extremely shrunken, spotted fruit, this year we've decided to allow the tree to blossom for cross-pollination, but thin all the fruit.

Sometimes, you can solve those cosmetic problems by focusing on different varieties. Consider potatoes. I love Yukons, but some of the spuds I grow can end up pretty scabby, and some, *really* scabby. And definitely look homely and unappetizing next to a grocery-store organic potato. So, I just cut around the spots. John likes russets, and the ones we've raised are mostly scab-free. As you see, there definitely are trade-offs.

## WILDLIFE PROVIDES BALANCE

Our neighborhood red-tailed hawks eat mice, the culprits who devour your fruit tree roots. But hawks and the other many raptors in the Foothills also eat chickens, and in fact, killed one of ours. You might not like garter snakes in your garden, but I've found they help keep down the vole population. Keeping a balanced, sustainable garden encourages critters like amphibians; toads especially eat mosquitoes. Since they like to bury themselves in the soil, you may be startled, though, when you reach for what looks like a spotted rock and it turns out to be a large toad!

Working with nature can also mean being okay with weeds where you don't want them. Early on, we thought beauty bark was the solution to pretty garden beds—only to learn that it works **against nature:** this store-bought amendment degrades nitrogen and other nutrients in the soil. Plus as it breaks down, it eventually turns into soil that's still too unproductive for veggies, and weeds soon grow in it anyway.

An alternative: wood chips made of ground-up wood and brush for mulch, as well as weed control on paths. It's also a great soil amendment for blueberry shrubs. John and I bought a wood-chipper some years ago, and it's turned out to be a wise investment.

Lots of people in our area spray their gravel driveways with Roundup. I shake my head, because 1) Roundup is more effective on "weaker links" like cultivated plants, and 2) the weeds always win and grow back anyway.

# SELECTING CROPS FOR YOUR HOMESTEAD GARDEN

*❦*

*B*y now, you hopefully have some ideas for 1) a site for your garden, 2) considering your permanent plantings and planning beds for annual produce, and 3) plants to encourage pollinators in your garden too. Ready for Step 4: raising food!

Here are some elements to consider for choosing your homestead-style garden crops:

**Plant what you like to eat.**

This, for me, is one of the most important criteria! For example, in previous years, I'd read radishes were a helpful "quick-crop" to plant in your parsnip bed, to shade the tiny, vulnerable parsnip seedlings. Radishes were back in style with trendy chefs, so we thought, why not? The radishes came up fast as advertised, and their foliage did shade the seedlings. Problem: neither John nor I like radishes. After many cooking experiments, all of them unsuccessful, we tossed the rest of the crop into the compost pile.

We did the same thing with arugula. I'd tried it in a restaurant and found it bitter, but hey, it's so good for you! So I planted a bed, found that it was indeed, very bitter. Into the compost went the arugula too.

**Plant what's easy to grow.**

Rhubarb is so easy it's perfect for the homestead garden. Since organic rhubarb can be $4 a pound in the store, it's a no brainer. Garlic too—like rhubarb, you just give it lots of compost and mulch and let it do its thing.

John and I love sweet potatoes and peppers, and they're so healthy too! We'd read about sweet potato varieties that can grow in cool climates, so we bought a bunch of (expensive) seed and planted away. All we could produce were these shrunken, sad little sweet potatoes. It's just not consistently warm enough in our climate.

The same goes for peppers. In our climate, in a really good year—that is, when we have a hot, dry summer—they'll produce. But we stopped buying starts because most years they just sat in the soil and looked droopy, and the blossoms didn't set.

**Plant what you really like but is too pricey to buy organic.**

Asparagus comes to mind. It's pretty high-maintenance to start, with trenching, weeding, picking every day during the harvest, then cleaning up the gigantic stalks in the winter and figuring out what to do with the piles of asparagus "straw"! But at 6.99/lb for organic, asparagus is more than worth it. Organic garlic at our local co-op is $9.95 a pound, so for me, growing garlic is an easy decision too.

Organic potatoes? 'Nuff said.

**Plant what suits your climate, and which has the best chance to thrive:**

The best veggies for our damp, cool, short-season climate have definitely been root crops! We have had consistently excellent results with garlic, carrots, and parsnips. However, purple and rainbow carrots didn't work; the ends decomposed, and there seemed to be lots of pest pressure all over the root.

In terms of warm weather crops like tomatoes and winter squash, here in the Foothills, many years have been a wash. So I've focused on tomato varieties with smaller fruits that are more suited to a cooler climate. The same with squash: large winter squash varieties just aren't consistent, so we've tried the smaller ones.

**Plant varieties that accommodate your personal tolerance for bugs/pests:**

You probably want to consider this when you're growing without pesticides. Cruciferous vegetables are very vulnerable to cabbage moths/worms; I discovered this our second year, when I tried to raise Brusse sprouts organically. I've NEVER seen so many green worms. To grow organic, you'll probably need row cover: lightweight, translucent polyester fabric you drape over beds and secure with rocks or other means to keep the moths out.

**Plant according to your tolerance for aesthetics:**

We covered this above: homestead potatoes and apples, grown without chemicals, will likely have scab, spots, and bugs to some degree. Conventionally-grown apples are also on the "dirty dozen" list of produce. On the other hand, home gardeners not spraying pesticides may have to deal with coddling moth and apple maggot.

John and I have been dealing with apple maggot for several years. It's a fly that lays eggs on the young apples, and when the eggs hatch, the larvae tunnel through the apples. The first year damage showed up in our apples, it was mostly aesthetic—some slight discoloration, nothing too yucky. We simply cut around the unsavory-looking parts. But over the next two or three seasons much of our fruit became inedible. Last year, we threw out all but about a dozen apples.

This season, John and I are trying a new three-prong intervention with 1) nematodes for the ground to inhibit the maggot pupa, 2) sticky traps in the trees to catch the flies, and 3) apple "booties" on the fruit to keep the larvae from tunneling in. I'll post the results on my blog at harvest time this coming summer and fall.

**Consider any extra effort for crops you're selecting:**

If you're set on producing a bumper crop of tomatoes every year in a cool climate, that may mean building a hoophouse or greenhouse. Are you up for the expense, time, and regular maintenance? How about repairs from weather damage?

Perhaps you are committed to growing organic, and are also willing to use sprays/interventions that are USDA-allowed for organic produce. Are you also up for the expense and time commitment, and the research required? For example, in terms of fruit trees, a lot of these interventions only work if you follow the protocols on a strict timetable in terms of blossom or fruit set.

It might come down to your own personal willingness to go through the extra work. Regarding our apple maggot problem, John and I put off dealing with the issue for years—we were being overly optimistic, "hoping" the maggots would go away. Now, after facing our two possibilities, either giving up raising apples and cutting down our trees, or putting in the effort to save our orchard, we're choosing our orchard and our commitment to self-reliance.

**Plant what you have room for.**

I've read many books and articles discussing how you can grow "x" amount of food in a small space. However, giving your food crops plenty of room means more water and nutrients are available for each plant. In my experience, more space really does mean better production.

Food crops that require lots of space besides fruit trees: corn and winter squash. With corn, which pollinates via wind carrying the pollen from plant to plant, you'll need a minimum number of plants or rows for successful pollination of the entire crop.

Winter squash vines can grow as long as 12 to 20 feet, and set additional roots in the soil along the length of the vine. Again, big plants need plenty of room to stretch out in to produce a viable crop.

I mentioned previously that I've found installing small beds, "pocket plots," around larger plants gives you a poor result. Larger plants like cruciferous crops (cabbage family) require lots of room to thrive as well. Early on, I made the mistake of planting potatoes in the same bed as broccoli. As I learned, both grow into large plants, and in a shared bed neither crop thrived.

Also in terms of gardening space, do you have ample room in your homestead garden to rotate your beds? If you're committed to raising your produce sustainably, crop rotation will help reduce the need for fertilizers, as well as reduce pests and funguses. More on crop rotation in the next chapter!

# CROP ROTATION: SOME GENERAL GUIDELINES

*a*s you select plants for your garden, bed rotation is an important tool for successful food-growing.

I raise tomatoes and potatoes every year. However, both belong to the same plant family (solanums or "nightshade") and are vulnerable to funguses like blight. The goal is to avoid planting either tomatoes or potatoes in same bed for 4 years. So you'll need to track both separate beds for each crop and avoid cross-rotation.

In cool, damp climates, fungus, including blight, presents a real challenge. In our county, seed potatoes are grown about 20 miles west of us. Fungus is transported through wind drift, so with the summertime prevailing winds coming from the west, blight at our place is inevitable. Even with careful rotation, we still end up seeing blight in both tomatoes and potatoes. However, since I began rotating both crops many years ago, the plants are impacted far less.

In addition to crop rotation, providing ample space between plants—which provides more air circulation—can also reduce blight.

The necessity of crop rotation isn't only because of fungus.

Different crops require different amounts and types of nutrients. So it's a good idea to alternate beds with "heavy feeders" like garlic with "light feeders" like legumes. Legumes (also called pulses) like peas and beans are considered "nitrogen fixing"—as I understand it, these plants have roots with little nodules that help the uptake of nitrogen to the soil.

Consider rotation in terms of plant "families":

We discussed above that tomatoes and potatoes are in the same plant family. Here are some others: 1) Cruciferous veggies: broccoli, cabbage, cauliflower, kale, and one that surprised me, turnips. 2) Alliums: garlic, onion, shallot. 3) Another family includes carrots, parsnips and celery, and herbs like parsley and dill. 4) Beets, spinach, and chard are also in the same family.

One tip I learned from the manager of our local Foothills nursery: she created a map of her garden beds, and each year, makes a note of her crops' locations. At any rate, rotating your crops contributes to a vibrant and diverse garden!

# A RESILIENT FOOD GARDEN:
## VEGETABLES AND HERBS

∞

*Y*our best chance to succeed at food self-reliance depends on creating a resilient garden, producing a harvest you can count on year in and year out. Especially if the unthinkable happens...

While experts say our current food supply is stable, what if our agricultural systems and grocery distribution goes sideways? Or becomes patchy? Selecting crops for self-reliance and resilience becomes critical. You may want to focus on crops that you can store, and/or crops that will sustain you with lots of protein, vitamins and calories.

According to author Carol Deppe, author of *The Resilient Gardener,* the best choices to provide necessary nutrition are corn, beans (dried), winter squash, potatoes, and eggs. You can store some of these crops for months, or in the case of "flint" corn (grown for flour) or beans, even years. Fresh eggs will keep for several months too. Deppe discusses this in detail in her book, which I highly recommend! (See the end of this guide for Deppe's book and more resources.)

## VEGETABLES

Potatoes are a great example of a resilient food source: pound for pound, they are high in vitamins and calories. There's a reason the Irish peasantry lived off potatoes for centuries. They were only allowed small plots, but a small field could produce many pounds of nutritious food.

In some areas, you can leave potatoes in the ground throughout the fall, which makes this crop doubly resilient. However, in a climate like ours, they'll need harvesting by the time fall rains start. There are exceptions: just yesterday, I pulled three overwintered russet potatoes out of last season's bed.

Also for resilience, consider selecting some wintering-over crops. Even in the harshest winters in the Foothills, parsnips, spinach, and sometimes carrots can overwinter. I have one parsley plant that has made it through despite an unusually harsh northeaster this past January.

As gardeners, most of us like to mix it up with some experimentation—trying new crop varieties or hybrids is part of the fun. But for the homestead garden, when feeding yourself and your family is the goal, you may want to stick with the tried-and-true. Keep in mind that selecting crops that have thrived in your particular climate for several successive seasons means optimal resilience.

In my experience, the following crops have grown easily in our climate and need little intervention or special treatment:

**Root Crops:**

Carrots: Nantes-type are shorter carrots, and need less time to mature. We sow one crop in spring for summer harvest and a second in early or mid-July to pick in fall.

Parsnips: Interesting fact: parsnips were a dietary mainstay in Northern Europe back in the day, before potatoes were brought back from the New World! They too are a complex carbohydrate with lots of nutrition. Aim to harvest any wintered-over parsnips by the end of February or so; if you leave them in the ground as spring approaches, the tops start to regrow. That fresh greenery is the start of a seed stalk, and the roots begin to turn bitter.

Potatoes (organic seed potatoes): Aim for high-quality seed with lots of "eyes."

Barbara Kingsolver sprouted her own homegrown potatoes for seed, but her climate may not be as affected by blight. Last year, I had problems sourcing seed potatoes, so I used "regular" organic potatoes from the produce department of my local co-op. Still, commercially raised seed potatoes may be more reliable, since they've been stored with certain protocols to aid in sprouting.

In terms of scab and other fungus, we've had the best success with russet (baking) varieties. Russets seem to be more resilient when it comes to cold, heat and too much rain or not enough. However, I love Yukon golds so I raise them too.

Beets: I prefer the Cylindra variety. The roots are more oblong than round, and are easier to peel.

Garlic: you can buy "seed" from your local nursery, but I have had five years of successful harvests buying locally-grown garlic from our co-op's produce department. I've been sticking with hard-neck garlic—it's generally more flavorful than soft neck, and that's what the local growers seem to raise. However, you can braid soft neck varieties for storage, and I've read that it keeps better.

Onion: I have found yellow onion is more resilient than red in terms of tolerating fluctuating temperatures and cooler weather. I've been buying local nursery seedlings, but "sets" (small bulbs) may be more reliable. Most years, I've planted the seedlings in May with mixed results. Last year, however, after planting in April I had a crop of large bulbs. This spring, I also planted in April, and this crop likewise has thrived. Clearly, an earlier planting leads to success!

**Spring Plantings:**

Peas: shelling, sugar snap, snow. Sow in early spring for best results; peas don't thrive in heat.

Swiss chard grows prolifically! The rainbow varieties add a nice color to your veggie garden.

Spinach is very reliable. I've had excellent results with the "Bloomsdale" variety: it's slow to bolt and readily overwinters. I sow it in early April and enjoy spinach salad throughout late spring!

With the heat of mid-summer, the plants start to bolt—that is, send up a seed stalk. If you let the seeds develop you can harvest them for a late summer planting. I try to plant my second spinach crop by early to mid-August, so there's some significant leaf growth before the first frost. Seedlings don't overwinter all that well, but here in the Foothills, the plants with one-or two-inch leaves tend to overwinter successfully, and you'll get a harvest the following spring.

**Warm Weather Crops:**

Cucumbers: We've had good results with "Marketmore," which I direct seed during the first warm spell in June. They work great for salads and refrigerator pickles too. These cukes seem to tolerate a little cool weather and will keep going well into September.

Zucchini or summer squash: I always grow Costata Romanesco, a light-green, striped heirloom. This type has a more complex flavor than the standard dark green varieties. John likes the deep green zucchinis so we plant both. If you are a huge zucchini fan, the lemon cultivar is smaller but can bear prolifically!

Winter squash: Delicata bears smaller fruits and is fairly reliable in our climate so we sow a bed every year. As I mentioned, our season here has proved to be too short for larger varieties to ripen before the first frost. Our best success raising other varieties (before we gave up) was with Blue Hubbards, buttercup, and some heirlooms.

Tomatoes: In our climate, varieties producing smaller fruits provide the best chance of ripening before the blight starts around mid-August. After many years of trying various kinds, we've had best success with "Stupice," "Sweet Million" cherry, and "Juliet," a small, pear-shaped roma. "Muskvich," a larger slicing variety, and Early Girl" have done well in our warmest summers, when we have heat well into late September.

Every few years we'll have a noticeably cooler summer, and our tomato crop has been pretty much of a bust: only a few tomatoes will ripen. Several of my students report that they've had success ripening their green tomatoes with the following: Wrap each one separately in newspaper, then place in a box also lined with newspaper and store in a dark location. My own experience: if our area has a cool, rainy late summer, blight starts spoiling the green tomatoes before you pick them, and they'll decompose even with the newspaper trick.

Some crops that haven't worked particularly well for us:

John and I have tried to grow lettuce, green beans, and shelling beans for drying, without producing much of a crop.

Lettuce problem: we'll often have a stretch of cool weather in late spring, then a sudden hot spell with temperatures in the 80s. The plants start developing a seed spike within a day, and once they start bolting even a little, the lettuce turns very bitter.

Green beans and dried beans: At our place, just when they're ripening around mid-August, our nights turn chilly, and sometimes dip into the 30s. The tips of the beans turn brown. So we have pretty much given up on beans.

## HERBS: HARDY AND ANNUAL

**Perennials:**

Hardy varieties are a great addition to your homestead garden. I previously mentioned raising perennial herbs for pollinating your crops, but if you're not interested in a lot of store-bought spices and seasonings, herbs will do triple duty: they add flavor to your cooking, they reliably grow year after year, and the highly aromatic ones can help repel some insect pests!

Perennial herbs are generally drought tolerant—helpful for our dry late summers in the Foothills. Here are our most successful hardy herbs:

Oregano: But you have watch it; oregano can be very invasive, since it reproduces by both runners and seeds. We brought **one** pot of oregano from our city garden, and now it's expanded all around our cleared acre.

Mints: Peppermint and spearmint. We've tried more "exotic" cultivars like chocolate mint and pineapple mint but they gave up the ghost after a season or two. Mint smells divine and bees love it, but it's also invasive.

Thyme: reseeds readily.

Lavender: also reseeds. We find volunteers all over our garden.

Sage: Can grow at least a foot each season! And bees LOVE the flowers.

Tarragon: Our one plant has survived for years, even surrounded on all sides by aggressive oregano volunteers. John snips a few leaves now and then, but I think it's an acquired taste.

Rosemary: This pretty, upright herb loves heat. We had one in the city that succumbed to cold, but we planted one here next to our south-facing house foundation and it has thrived for three years. Plus rosemary doesn't need annual pruning like lavender and oregano.

Lovage: We planted two lovage starts after a friend recommended it as a celery substitute. Problem: when I put even a few leaves in some vegetable soup, the herb was so highly aromatic, like celery times 10, that's all I could taste. Plus within about three months, both plants were over five feet tall! It might be a reliable choice, but lovage didn't work for us. So out it came, and not easily!

**Annual herbs:**

Cilantro: readily reseeds, and tiny wasps love the flowers. By late summer, we'll have cilantro volunteers all over the garden, and they tolerate cool weather well. The plants die with the first hard frost, so it's all good!

Basil: There's nothing even close to homegrown, fresh-picked basil for your pesto! But basil is not at all hardy. I grow two or three nursery starts in black pots right next to the south-facing foundation of our house, and it's still not warm enough. By early August, the foliage turns pale and the flavor diminishes. So use it up while the leaves are still deep green.

Dill: It can reseed like crazy. Over a three-year period, one dill plant near my asparagus has reseeded throughout the whole bed. And shown up in many other raised beds! One of my students joked there's a reason it's original name is "dillweed."

Parsley: I've had good luck with the flat-leaf variety, which will keep growing even after the first frost. Wonderful flavoring for soups and stews! Rabbits like it, so give it some protection.

Highly-scented herbs can also repel pests, as I mentioned. Plant them near your beds, but not in! Marigold is not officially an herb but can also repel pests. I've read it's especially helpful to plant as a companion to tomatoes.

# A RESILIENT FOOD GARDEN:
## FRUIT

## BERRIES AND FRUIT TREES

*A* variety of berries are a wonderful choice for a year-after-year food supply, but nurturing berry plants for a successful harvest does take some effort. However, **strawberries and blueberries,** to me, are too delicious **not** to grow!

### STRAWBERRIES

Raising strawberry plants is pretty straightforward: try to get your new strawberry crowns or starts in the ground by mid-spring, so the plant's root system can get well established by the time the summer heat arrives. As with all your food crops, planting in soil with lots of organic material is optimal. I always work in a generous amount of compost, and after planting, I top dress the bed with mulch like leaves.

That first spring, it's a good idea to pick off all the flower buds so each plant's energy goes into the root system—thus creating bigger, healthier berries down the road. The berries are then ready for harvesting the second year.

As I mentioned previously, a strawberry plant will bear for only a few years. Thus, to have a continual harvest, you might plan to establish a new patch with fresh starts every couple of years or so.

The real effort is in protecting your crops! Both strawberries and blueberries require intensive netting. Rabbits eat the strawberry foliage, especially the emerging leaves at the crown. They also chomp on blueberry plants, particularly the more tender new growth. Pretty much every home gardener must net both crops against birds; at our place, we've had chipmunks, voles, and mice devour our strawberry and blueberry crop.

### BLUEBERRIES:

Blueberries are among the easiest to grow (if not net) for the homestead gardener: plant two or more varieties for cross-pollinizing. (Note: pollinizers are plants, the source of the pollen, while pollinators are the bees and other critters that move the pollen around.) As with strawberries, you'll give your plants the best start if you pick off all the flowers the first year.

Confession: early in the homestead gardening game, John and I could not bring ourselves to pick off the blueberry flowers —we were in too much of a hurry to eat our own blueberry crop. Now I wonder how much more vigorous our plants might have been if we'd followed that advice!

I prefer the taller cultivars, since I'd rather pick berries standing up than crouching! Blueberries do require acidic soil but generally don't need any added nitrogen. If you want to use fertilizer, try the kind that's formulated for berries and other acid-loving crops, and avoid using fertilizers meant for your vegetable garden.

Blueberry shrubs do best with an annual pruning—in our region, it's recommended that you prune them in April, when the plants are in flower. Without pruning, they may overbear, which can affect future harvests. There's a technique to pruning blueberry shrubs, so if you're new at it, for the best results you might consider consulting your local nursery staff or your favorite garden resources online or in books.

For a couple of years, I was reluctant to prune my blueberry shrubs, since it involved losing some berries! But after a rabbit got into our blueberry patch and chomped on one shrub—severely pruning it for us—I realized pruning really was good for the bushes: this shrub turned into the most vigorous one in the patch!

Armed with this new insight, I really got into the spirit of pruning. Here's my routine: I watch for the first swelling of flower buds, which in the Foothills, happens around early April. If you wait too long to prune, the flowers will be starting to open, and are more vulnerable to being accidentally jostled or knocked off the plant while you're pruning.

My own strategy is to prune away dead wood first, including dead twigs or ends. Then I trim out any weak or super-skinny canes that don't have many flowers on them. Trimming the top section of new, long canes can help force side growth and buds for next year's berries. Keep in mind it's the colored wood (not the branches with gray bark) that sets the buds for more side shoots!

Pruning blueberries has actually become one of my favorite food-garden tasks. The first sunny, mild day in April, I'll take a little stool and my smallest pruning scissors into the berry patch and settle in. As I trim away at the bushes, I really get into the zone, or maybe the Zen of it, and the hours fly by. It's good for inner peace!

Again, I also recommend that you get a little instruction before pruning.

Because blueberry shrubs have a lot of surface roots, mulching is highly recommended to keep the roots moist between watering (during the summer, they need 1 inch of water per week). Before we got a wood chipper, I used sawdust on the soil beneath each bush. But now, with an ample supply of wood chips on hand, I use generous amounts, mixed with coffee grounds if I have them, for top-dressing each plant to the drip line. In our climate, with frequent stretches of dry weather from July through September, blueberry mulch is particularly essential.

Mulch in your blueberry patch also helps prevent mummy-berry disease. It's a fungus that attacks blueberry shrubs, causing the berries to shrivel up and turn white. I'd heard of mummyberry many years ago, but wasn't really sure what it was or what it looked like. I'd also seen a ton of shriveled berries at a poorly maintained U-pick blueberry farm, but I thought maybe these deformed berries were due to insufficient water.

Then came my wake-up call a couple of years ago. It happened in late June, just as my two blueberry patches were showing lots of healthy fruit set. The clusters were bursting with swelling white berries, taking on a bluish tinge—the first sign of ripening. As with previous seasons, I pictured the bowls of fresh berries we'd eat, the gallons of berries I'd process for the deep-freeze.

As the days went by, I encountered a head-scratcher: shrubs that previously had been laden with berries looked...emptier. I'd find berry stems with no berries on them, as if the robins had been gobbling them. But the nets were secure, and besides, robins are too smart to eat white berries—they wait until the berries are blue and sweet, and then start attacking them.

More days passed. Most of my blueberry bushes now held only a middling amount of berries—I'd never seen this before. The fruit seemed to be disappearing before my very eyes. Poking around the shrubs, it was then I saw them: shriveled grayish-white bits on the ground, bits that used to be blue-berries.

I'd seen a few of these tiny shriveled berries on my shrubs before—I figured it was nature's way of preventing the blue-berry shrubs from working too hard. But this year, there were way too many to ignore. And many, many berries still on the bush were half-wrinkled, and turning a sickly purple. You'd barely touch them and they'd fall off the stem. Something was definitely *wrong*.

IN MY POLLYANNA WAY, I'd figured mummyberry was something only *other* growers got. After all, I'd faithfully mulched my berry shrubs to prevent it—along with meticulous pruning and watering, my berries got the best of care. But when the numbers of shriveled bits were too alarming to ignore, I made myself Google mummyberry disease.

And sure enough, that's what we had. With this particular fungus, the afflicted berries fall off the shrub, looking "mummified." But it gets worse. If you don't pick all your little "mummies" off the bush or the ground, each one develops into this mushroom-like thingy in the fall. I read that this tiny puffball will release thousands of spores in late winter. Then the spores re-infect your shrub and set you up for a worse fungal attack the next year.

Well, if cleaning up the berries was what it took, that's what I'd do. That summer, I crawled under the berry nets each day and picked up every last one of those little suckers. I then threw the "mummies" in the trash, not the compost pile. In the years since, I've continued the practice, and seen a huge improvement.

Some organic commercial blueberry growers, including a local grower we talk to regularly, install their shrubs in raised rows covered with industrial-strength weed barrier, with grass between the rows. I asked our grower acquaintance about this practice, and she said that with the weed barrier, the shriveled berries will easily roll away from the bushes and into the grass. Then each day of the season, they run a vacuum between the rows!

Back to **mulching**: when you mulch your blueberry shrubs in the spring, pull back the old mulch (this way, any mummies will get buried in the mulch) before you apply a fresh layer. The goal for mummyberry control is to make sure the soil around the shrub is well covered.

One blueberry pest I've noticed around mid-spring: small green worms about the size of a fingernail clipping will wrap themselves inside a leaf, then eat the stems of a berry cluster. The result is an entire cluster will die and crumble away. The worm, if left to develop, turns into a little brown pupa, and will hatch and return to do more damage next year! So every once in a while, inspect your shrubs for curled leaves, and you find the worm or pupa, tear off the leaf and dispose of it in the trash.

## Cane berries

John and I have found cane berries like marionberries, raspberries, tayberries, loganberries and boysenberries have less pressure from wildlife than strawberries and blueberries. And they're delicious!

Tayberries are the earliest caneberries, and have delicious flavor. However, the berries are very delicate and will ripen and spoil quickly on the cane. So be prepared to pick every day!

Our favorite cane berries are by far marionberries, a blackberry cultivar. Year after year, they've proven to be the most reliable, abundant, and tasty of all the cane berries. They aren't immune from pests, however. As the harvest begins to wane, the ants start wandering all over the berries. Once they've pierced any berries, releasing some juice, then the hornets move in. Loganberries are another delicious choice, but they need to be picked just at ripening, or the berry quality goes downhill pretty quickly. For all cane berries, it's important to cut away any spent canes after they're done bearing, so the plant can put its energy into the new, emerging canes that will bear next year's crop.

## Huckleberries

We planted three evergreen huckleberry bushes in shady spots, and they have produced an abundant crop every year since they began bearing. You do have to be very patient to pick huckleberries, since the fruit is so tiny! Birds love them, so be prepared to share as well. We also have a high-country huckleberry, a smallish variety that hasn't produced much of a crop. This huckleberry isn't quite as hardy as the evergreens; a severe cold snap tends to damage the plant but it has always bounced back. Rabbits will eat both the twigs and branches, so make sure you install protection.

### BERRY EXPERIMENTS

We planted a **justaberry** bush in the corner of one of our orchards, and it hasn't grown particularly well. Additionally, the fruit is tricky to pull off off the bush, plus it has a strange "hairy" coating that is very high maintenance for processing. So we basically let the birds have the fruit.

After hearing about the anti-viral and immune-building qualities of **elderberry**, this week, John purchased and planted two bare-root elderberry plants. We'll see how easy the plants are to grow and what kind of crop they produce!

## FRUIT TREES AND OTHER FRUIT

For fresh eating apples, we've had very little scab with Akane, Elstar, Florina, Honeycrisp, William's Pride, and Centennial crabapple (a sweet variety). These varieties have also provided a steady harvest: Williams Pride and Centennial in August, Akane in early September, Honeycrisp later in September, Elstar early October, and Florina, late October. Our Gravenstein does get some scab that's not too overwhelming. John had his heart set on Jonagold, so we got one. Which sad to say, gets pretty scabby.

**For storage**, don't wait until apples fall from the tree: harvest the fruit before it's fully ripe.

**Making cider?** Heirloom and otherwise old-fashioned apple varieties can provide more complex flavor.

**Asian pear:** A very abundant and reliable crop! Our one Asian pear tree self-pollinizes (meaning it's self-fertile) and grows several feet each year, so be prepared to prune well each spring. The fruit is somewhat delicate, and not particularly good for storage. John likes to mix Asian pear with apples for his homemade applesauce.

**Other fruit:**

**Kiwi:** Ah yes, another experiment. You need a male and a female kiwi, so we planted both. The female grew like crazy, producing vines 10 feet long each season. We kept this pair for about seven years without a sign of any fruit. Finally, we decided we'd been patient enough, and took the kiwis out.

**Grapes:** need intensive netting and a warm growing season. We originally planted three grapevines and discovered the blue-jays generally hit the grapes before they're fully ripe. As with the marionberries, with the scent of juice wafting in the air, in come the hornets!

One of our three grapevines was located next to a food-growing area, and the nearby crops didn't do particularly well. Then I discovered the ginormous root system of the grapevine beneath those beds. While the vine provided lots of welcome shade, it went the way of the fig, the kiwis and our other non-successful experiments: we took it out. And after much gnashing of teeth over the bird predation of the remaining two grape plants, John and I basically grow them for shade.

By now, you've probably seen that at our place, any plant

that 1) doesn't really thrive, 2) earn its keep with a fairly decent harvest, or 3) at least feed the wildlife, gets jettisoned. When you're growing food you're counting on, sometimes you have to be ruthless. But I've concluded a garden system works best when you have healthy plants that can provide a healthy harvest. Like a rising tide that lifts all boats: a healthy plant enhances the health of the soil and plants around it.

And after our many failed fruit experiments, I've pretty much concluded you have the most success by sticking with the basics!

# MORE CULTIVATION TIPS FOR A
# SUCCESSFUL HARVEST

*M*any homestead gardeners get an early start to the growing season by starting seeds indoors, particularly crops that require a long ripening season like tomatoes and winter squash. John and I have not gone that route. Despite having lots of windows on the south side of our house, we simply don't have the room. Also, our south-facing windows are next to the woodstove, and it would be too hot for tender seedlings.

Additionally, plants started indoors need serious hardening off before planting, and our climate is too unpredictable. John and I have developed the attitude that any crops we start from seed have to germinate outside, survive **and** bear a crop, or not at all. As I mentioned, I buy almost all our seeds from local growers. (I haven't found Cylindra beet and organic parsnip seed locally, so I source them from organic companies out of the area.)

Root crops need to be directly seeded in the ground. Squash can get started in pots, but keep in mind they can have serious transplant shock. We always just wait until soil warms and direct seed.

Lots of warm weather crops will germinate in cool soil… but not necessarily mature! I made the mistake of tossing my immature or past their prime winter squash on the compost pile. The next growing season, after liberally spreading that compost around the garden, I had to pull squash seedlings out of the beds all summer. The same goes for tomato seeds, which will readily germinate in cool weather. But our season isn't nearly long enough for the small seedlings to grow to harvest. Instead, I buy organic tomato plants in ½ gallon pots for the best chance of a crop before the blight hits.

An easy rule of thumb: for optimal yields of all plants, **keep beds moist and weeded** so there's less stress and/or competition for individual plants. I've also learned this the hard way: slacking on weeding resulted in lower production. Keep in mind that stressed plants are more vulnerable to pests and fungus too.

**A successful harvest can depend on adequate structures where needed.**

Berries: I've discussed netting previously. For our strawberries, we must weigh down the nets with stones or chunks of lumber to keep out the chipmunks. Netting for blueberries is also essential: Chipmunks, mice, robins, and towhees go after the berries; goldfinch especially are relentless, and will fly right through one-inch wire.

Peas: Towhees will pluck newly sprouted pea seeds right out of the soil, so we must net our pea seedlings until they're a few inches tall. Peas are much happier with staking—better air circulation means less powdery mildew. Plus, with staking, it's easier to pick your crop, and regularly picking your peas will result in a longer harvest. If you neglect to pick them for a few days, the plant begins going to seed. Bush varieties are a little easier to manage without staking, but I've found they can still fall all over the beds. For staking, John cuts birch boughs from the woods and uses pea twine (string) to tie the boughs together.

Tomatoes: staking is essential for good ventilation/air circulation. Without staking, non-determinate varieties, which just keep growing until frost, will collapse in a heap. Also, staking helps keep fruit from sitting directly on the soil, which helps prevent blight from taking over. You can buy tomato cages, which to me seem awfully small for most tomato plants, but John gets good results from his strategy of tree boughs and string. Also, these homemade structures are easy to add on to as the plant increases in size!

Cattle or stock panels can be really handy for heavy-foliaged climbers. I recommend them for staking beans, and some folks use it for cucumbers. While birch boughs will start breaking down after one season, stock panels are useable year after year.

**You can find tips for cultivating several crops on my blog,** www.littlefarminthefoothills.blogspot.com

# A CHEMICAL-FREE HOMESTEAD GARDEN

❧

lthough the fertilizer and gardening aids companies would like us to believe their products are absolutely essential, you *can* produce a successful harvest in a chemical-free food garden! To avoid using commercial garden products like pesticides, herbicides, fertilizers and fungicides, let's revisit a theme I mentioned previously: **Working with nature.**

### Avoiding pesticide use

We discussed previously that crop rotation is one very effective way to keep pest populations down. Keep in mind that certain bugs attack certain plants (squash bugs, carrot flies, aphids, etc.). By swapping out your crop to new location, bugs can't settle in for long-term.

Also, you can aim for that balanced garden we discussed earlier: a wide variety of native plants and pollinators can encourage pest-eating insects and other wildlife to make their homes in your garden. Once you use bug spray, it upsets the natural balance and can have a cascading effect: you can get rid of one pest and get infested with another. Most certainly, bug spray will kill lots of bees and other pollinators.

If you do get a pest infestation, you can avoid pesticide use by the manual method: you can hand-pick larger bugs, or spray aphids with water, etc.

### Avoiding fertilizer use

We don't use store-bought fertilizer; chemical fertilizers generally feed the plants, not the soil. In fact, those chemicals that encourage plant growth can deplete soil over time. As I understand it, chemical fertilizers create "salts" in soil, and without organic material to feed on, the microbes will then take the nutrients they need from the soil—leaving less for the plants.

### Avoiding herbicide use

Killing weeds with herbicide will impact food crops' soil fertility for possibly many growing seasons. Or poison your soil outright. And there's always the worry of herbicide collateral damage to wildlife. While weeding by hand is probably the hardest work you ever have to do in your food garden, there are ways to keep weeds to a minimum. Or, at least prevent them from taking over!

Happily, you can utilize homemade methods to both **control weeds and fertilize your plants**, and at the same time, build your soil for a healthy food system. How does that work? Two words: **compost and mulch**.

In my experience, compost and mulch work hand in hand to enhance your soil and maintain fertility in your garden beds. To create both materials in the homestead-style garden, you can use what's readily on hand. Details in the next chapters!

# MULCH

Mulch is organic material you add on the surface of your garden beds: grass clippings, prunings, leaves, and wood chips (not beauty bark). Mulch provides myriad benefits: weed suppression, regulates soil temperatures, plants need less watering, and it reduces soil heaving in winter from frost and thaw cycles, to name a few. In our damp climate, we get a lot of moss invading beds where the soil isn't disturbed much, for example, the asparagus patch, and covering the moss with mulch helps keep it down.

**Leaves:** At our place, I create mulch from our deciduous tree leaves, especially the many native maples in the woods. Brackenfern grows prodigiously here, so I harvest a lot of that for mulch too. **(Avoid using fruit tree leaves and prunings in your mulch, since they carry funguses.)** Even if you have only one or two trees in your yard, the leaves can enhance your garden. So rake your leaves and protect the pile from wind, or if your neighbors have trees and you think they'll be game to share, ask them for their leaves!

We purchased a leaf-chipper (in addition to the wood chipper, a much more powerful machine) which has been hugely helpful and is easy for me to operate. Whole leaves, especially big leaf maple, are prone to fly off the garden beds in a brisk wind; one of our cold-weather northeasters will peel the leaf mulch right off the soil and fling it around the yard! Ground-up leaves are more likely to settle right into the soil and they'll break down faster too.

My favorite mulch is ground-up leaves weighed down with damp, homemade compost. (More about compost shortly.)

**Hay:** Some folks use hay for mulch. Hay is recently cut pasture grass, and is generally full of seed heads—so it needs to be composted (sit in a pile and turned occasionally to decompose) for many months.

**Newspaper and cardboard:** I use these non-organic materials to cover overwintering beds—it will prevent your planting areas filling with weeds by the time you're ready to sow seeds. It's also helpful when weeds have gotten upper hand in the fall: applying a paper mulch will eliminate the weeds by spring. An extra plus: the safe and moist environment beneath cardboard and newspaper also helps nurture earthworms.

A drawback: while covering beds with cardboard in the fall makes your food garden look tidy and well-maintained, by early spring, the cardboard will likely grow tatty. And when a stiff breeze comes along, you'll probably see bits of cardboard blowing around! However, I've decided that tatty cardboard is better than a garden overrun with weeds: although it can look pretty unsightly, you'll end up with a more productive and less labor-intensive garden!

**Wood chips** are a terrific way to suppress weeds between beds. As I mentioned above, you can directly mulch blueberries with wood chips; to apply to vegetable-growing areas, it's a good idea to compost your chips for at least a year or two.

Over time, using the materials I've mentioned in your garden beds, and any other organic materials you come up with, really helps build healthy, fertile soil!

However, mulch can be a mixed blessing: it provides an excellent cover for voles and the mice using their tunnels. My goal is to find a balance. Also, I occasionally stick a spading fork in my mulched areas, in hopes of destroying their tunnels!

Mulch can also keep soil too cool for planting in spring. So a week or two before I'm ready to sow seeds, I remove the mulch and set it aside, and hope the weeds don't move in. After the seedlings are up, I spread the mulch back on the beds for moisture and weed control. Take care, however, to wait until the seedlings have a solid start! I have sometimes replaced the mulch too soon, and the towhees at our place have scratched at the mulch for bugs. The result: damaged seedlings and a reduced crop.

**SOME EARLY LESSONS with mulch and soil building:**

**Straw:** In earlier years, I used lots of straw for mulch to prevent weeds, both between larger plants, and for pathways between beds. Then I discovered from the wonderful staff at our local nursery that **straw is not the best option**: almost all straw comes from grain crops applied with herbicides. Also, straw has generally been dried in a kiln, and is basically sterile as a result. (Although some weed seeds do survive—that's weeds for you!) Unless you can source your straw from sustainably grown grain, my advice is to avoid.

**Beauty bark:** I mentioned previously that John and I were lured into using commercial beauty bark to cover bare soil—I mean, it makes your yard look great, doesn't it? Then we learned that beauty bark had a negative effect on soil: too much carbon, for one thing, and whatever dyes are used for the rich, redwood color can't help either. In a few spots in our garden, even 10 years after applying beauty bark, weeds grow like crazy, but the soil is still unsuitable for food growing. The soil, though, can rebound: I have pulled beauty bark off a few areas, added a lot of organic material, and over time, created a productive vegetable bed.

**Commercial mushroom compost:** It's called "mushroom" compost because this material has been used for growing mushrooms, but it's comprised mostly of chicken manure. Our second growing season, we purchased a truckload of commercial mushroom compost to amend some of our beds.

I came to regret this shortcut. We had large garden areas to cover, and wanted to increase our soil fertility in short amount of time. John and I bought this product before I knew much about sustainable gardening, or had even thought about it very much, and so I'd done no research before we purchased the three yards from a local gravel company.

In this compost, I found debris here and there, like small pieces of plastic, empty soda cans and other bits of trash. Hardly the "clean" sort of garden amendment I would have preferred! If your goal is a sustainable garden with minimal toxins, think backwards. Where did this product or manure come from? Were the chickens pastured, or raised indoors, crowded in cages? Where the birds fed with organic or GMO feed? Or feed from herbicide-sprayed crops or raised from Roundup Ready seed? Were animals given hormones or antibiotics? Whatever goes into a product like this will end up in your garden.

Keep in mind that mushroom compost and chicken manure, even composted, isn't really appropriate for berries, since it's highly alkaline. Berries generally like more acidic soil. And since blueberries require acidic soil to thrive, you should avoid using it altogether in your blueberry patch.

**Plastic "mulch."** A few years back, some areas of our food garden became completely overgrown by weeds. Without sufficient time and energy to weed by hand, I had John buy sheets of black plastic to cover those areas. I figured it was a win-win: Plastic can also warm the soil; in the past, I placed black plastic around tomato plants. (Note: little water will reach the plants, however.) Black plastic mulch was highly effective...until it wasn't.

I came to regret the plastic shortcut too, after making an unfortunate discovery: over time, the plastic that had been so helpful for smothering weeds had started to break down into shreds. This past fall, I spent many, many hours picking tiny shards of plastic out of the soil—time I could have put to better use.

# COMPOST

ompost, which is decomposed organic material, combines the best qualities of mulch and fertilizer. In my experience, it's also the quickest and easiest path to create and maintain healthy soil. Here's another one of our lessons:

John and I took another shortcut our first two years at Berryridge Farm with commercial steer manure compost. We bought many sacks of a locally-manufactured product to build our soil, particularly in our berry patches. It was expensive (I think about $10 per cubic foot) but it looked very healthy—dark, damp, and fluffy—and seemed to work well.

Then the news came out about a commercial brand of steer manure compost, made from cows that had grazed in pastures applied with Roundup or other herbicides. Some commercial growers in our county had used this particular product on a large scale. Most of their crops just shriveled away or died, and these growers lost years of production. Other growers' soil was completely poisoned. Since the product was made from many cows grazing on many fields in untraceable locations, how could you ever determine who truly was at fault?

For me, the overriding lesson has been that factory garden

shortcuts usually come back to bite you—it's better to stick to working with nature!

You can buy organic compost, but it's very expensive too. If it's possible, I recommend that you make your own.

I was reluctant at first to jump on the homemade compost bandwagon. Having bears in our neighborhood was a powerful deterrent. Then after our mushroom compost and steer compost experiments, I decided the risk of attracting bears was worth the reward. I started my own kitchen compost pile.

I was rewarded: our food-growing garden took a quantum leap in production after I started using my own compost and mulch in tandem. Keep in mind that it can take months to create a steady supply of compost, so there's no time like the present to get started.

My basic recipe is super simple: Nitrogen + Carbon. N = green material like kitchen scraps, plant tops, grass clippings (avoid using weeds because of the seeds). C = dry, crunchy materials: dry leaves, dead asparagus tops, brown brackenfern.

Composting homestead-style means you can create your compost in a hole, a trench, or inside a small, above-ground fenced spot, rather than buying a fancy compost container at a gardening supply store.

**How I make compost:**

I keep my own process basic and not terribly scientific: I balance green veggie waste (which is nitrogen-rich) with brown crunchy stuff (the carbonaceous element) and keep the pile mixed up. I recommend aiming to add to your compost year round—even in a moderately chilly winter climate like the Foothills, when the ground freezes frequently from November through March, the pile itself won't freeze solid if you turn it once or twice a week.

My composting site is a shallow hole about three feet across and 18 inches deep—it's more like a wide trench. Into the trench goes a bucket of soil, as weed-free and rock-free as I can make it, then a small pile of dried leaves and twigs for the bottom layer, to provide some air pockets. I top the soil and leaves with a bucket of kitchen scraps like raw veggie peelings and apple cores (again, the green stuff), then add another large bucket of dead leaves (the brown stuff).

Mix/turn well, and let nature do its magic. Every time I add food scraps to the pile, I also add old leaves or dead bracken-fern. In the summertime, when I might be putting lots of strawberry tops or other fruit scraps in my compost, the pile may grow acidic, so I make sure to add extra brown material.

Naturally, I had a compost learning curve along with all the others: For many years, I did have enough of a clue to discard our blighty tomato and potato foliage **only** in my weed piles out in the woods—**not** in my compost pile. But I was still adding spoiled or unusable potatoes and tomatoes to my compost. And despite rotating my beds religiously, I was still seeing lots of blight in the beds—and I became very discouraged. Then I had another one of my garden epiphanies. Those discarded tomatoes and taters were bringing funguses into the compost, and as a result blight was sure to develop in soil wherever I put it. It took several years for the funguses to wear out or decompose, but I'm seeing far less blight.

Depending on the blight and other fungus issues in your climate, you may also want to avoid putting discarded tomatoes, potatoes, or their peels into your pile too.

During dry periods, keep the pile moist. Try to turn your compost every time you add green material—it'll help keep the decomposition process more active. An added benefit to frequent turning: recognizable food chunks break down faster, thus attracting fewer rodents, other critters, and neighbor dogs!

Let your pile "cook" for a couple of months, until the food scraps and dead leaves have "digested" into a fairly uniform, rich, dark substance, then you're ready to spread the compost on your garden beds. The secret to a swift scraps-to-finished-compost process lies in a couple of factors: keep your kitchen scraps and peelings fairly small, and as I've said before, turn your pile often and well! There's a world of microbes doing their thing in there, and every time you turn your compost, you're introducing fresh oxygen into the pile.

With infrequent turning, you may not get enough oxygen into the pile, and it will soon get a very sour smell. That can mean the decomposition process is turning anaerobic, and all your microorganisms aren't getting the oxygen they need.

In terms of other high-nitrogen materials beyond fruit and veggie material, some gardeners might add grass clippings to the pile—a great choice, as long as you don't use "Weed n' Feed" or moss killer on your lawn. Others adhere to the "everything and the kitchen sink" philosophy, tossing in stuff like hair clippings, weeds, and newspaper. Personally, I keep my "ingredients" strictly food-related. Keep in mind that leftovers don't make optimal additives, especially meat or dairy products— you're likely to eventually find maggots in your pile. Also avoid fatty or oily food items as well.

Keep your compost pile active during winter by adding dry material regularly. While I till only minimally in my garden beds, I'm all for chopping and turning compost vigorously. If you keep up a regular compost-turning schedule, with all that activity you'll stay healthy too!

I actually keep two kitchen compost piles. I have one that I'm actively adding scraps to and turning regularly. My second compost pile I leave alone, with only occasional turning; it's finishing its "digestion" process, and will be ready for applying while the first pile is still "cooking" away!

You'll note that my kitchen compost pile is "vegetarian" compost, and I don't add chicken manure to it. That way, my compost is safe to put on my veggie beds, and I can also apply it to ground-sitting fruit like strawberries and cranberries in both spring and fall.

I keep our chicken manure in a different compost pile. We use wood chips for our coop and nest bedding, so the manure is mixed with generous amounts of woody material. Generally, I don't get around to turning the manure as frequently as my kitchen pile so it doesn't break down very fast. I use this manure on our asparagus beds in the fall. Otherwise, I let the chicken manure sit and decompose for many months before using in the vegetable beds.

# OTHER SOIL AMENDMENTS

*T*he one store-bought soil amendment we use is dolomite lime for our veggie beds. (Important: dolomite lime is NOT the caustic lime that's used in applications like concrete and to disinfect an outhouse trench.) With the ample rainfall in our area, our soils are generally acidic, which is why berries grow so well! However, most veggies do not thrive in acidic soil: lime "sweetens" the soil by adding alkaline. Dolomite lime comes in little pebble-sized granules and actually has a sweet odor.

A lot of gardening experts strongly recommend that you have your soil pH tested, especially before using dolomite lime. It's up to you. I use this lime fairly sparingly, and sprinkle it here and there on each vegetable bed in the fall, after the rains have started. After applying, I gently rake in the granules or rough up the soil with a hand trowel. Since potatoes like slightly acidic soil, I pre-select a potato bed in fall for spring planting, and don't add lime.

There are additional purchased soil amendments that can be beneficial. A few "natural" (as opposed to chemical) fertilizers can include: liquid fish fertilizer, kelp, and seed meal, such as alfalfa, cottonseed, etc. These products can all help stimulate soil microbes.

In addition to the composted manure that we discussed above, more made-from-nature fertilizer options include: peat moss; used, well-composted horse bedding; and grape crushings. You can chicken manure, but as I emphasized before, fresh manure is too strong/alkaline for seeds and seedlings.

I've heard of some people using small amounts of wood ash but I've never tried it. I use our woodstove ashes out in the woods to cover up any discarded potatoes, tomatoes or apples, to keep the bears from munching them!

**Another note about healthy soil:**

Not all the fungus in your garden is bad! In healthy, generally undisturbed soil, you'll find tiny white threads called Mycelium, which is a multi-celled "web" or network of beneficial fungal organisms. In a workshop at a local farm resource center, I learned that these fungi help decompose organic matter and feed on insects and other soil organisms. They also improve soil structure by binding soil particles to this web. The result is improved uptake of nutrients to your crops.

At our place, I'd noticed these threads when we'd first dug into forest soil years ago. Tilling your soil will break up this web, which can take 2-3 years to rebuild.

Personally, I till minimally if possible, especially in beds where I've seen lots of the tiny threads. Before planting in the spring, I'll insert a spading fork in the beds to gently open up the soil a little, since with all the rainfall in the Foothills, soil can get pretty compacted over the winter. Introducing some air pockets into the soil will help root crops like carrots and potatoes expand into the space they need underground.

# ONE LAST WORD ABOUT CHEMICAL-FREE GARDENING: PESTS

❧

**S**lugs: Any pest discussion for raising food in a moist climate (like the maritime Pacific Northwest) would not be complete without mentioning the bane of every gardener: slugs! They will mow down an entire bed of seedlings, and pretty much destroy much of your vegetable garden. John and I use a store-bought product: Iron sulfate pellets, which are appropriate for organic gardens, and are safe for pets and wildlife. Instead of poisoning the slugs on contact, the pellets apparently make slugs sick, and they sort of slink away and die.

This year we've had a super-rainy spring, and the slug population has been epic. Some evenings, I'll mosey through the orchards with a shovel and just spear every slug I see. Yucky, but effective!

**Tent caterpillars:** Also in the Pacific Northwest, somewhere along the line you'll encounter tent caterpillars. You won't find them every year—infestations occur on a multi-year cycle. But as a precaution, I suggest you at least keep an eye out for them each early spring.

Watch for their egg sacks on your fruit trees: small charcoal-gray nodules wrapped around twigs. If you find these sacs, cut the twig or branch they're wrapped around and burn it. If the sacs drop on the ground, the eggs will still hatch. Once they do, the tiny caterpillars will quickly grow into worm-sized mega-pests! They'll defoliate the host tree or plant, and quickly proceed to basically wreak havoc in your orchard and berry patches.

HERE IN THE FOOTHILLS, we endured two successive years of tent caterpillar plagues. Not infestations. **Plagues.**

It was the most horrific experience on our homestead by far, and I've related the gruesome details in my second memoir, *Little Farm Homegrown.* In a plague year, the caterpillars will completely defoliate your fruit trees and berry plants. You can spray with Bt, a bacteria-based pesticide, but according to our local agricultural extension office, Bt breaks down within a few days. Since the life cycle of the caterpillars is over 4 weeks, if you do the math, many sprayings would be necessary.

It wasn't an option for us. Our place is surrounded by dozens of acres of alder trees, which is the native target plant for the caterpillars. We might've sprayed our orchard, but we couldn't spray our entire woods, or the neighbors' trees. So to save our food garden, John and I had no choice but to fell the most severely infested trees in the woods adjacent to the yard. After cutting off the treetops, we pruned out the nests, which we did for about two months. Once the caterpillars began invading our yard in waves, we had to kill them by hand for 4-6 weeks.

There was a silver lining, if you can believe it. Nature, albeit on her own timeline, actually provides a balance. The native trees that have been attacked by caterpillars will develop some kind of virus in their leaves to sicken the invaders and break the infestation cycle. This occurred the third year of the infestation at our place—and finally the plague ended. The bad news is, these infestations apparently occur every 10 years. However, I'm not going to think about it until I have to.

To me, part of the homestead-style mindset is not worrying about future problems. You'll have to deal with whatever comes anyway, so don't go looking for trouble.

**Birds:** Happily, bird invaders are far easier to manage than insects—still, going chemical-free in your garden means you'll have lots of them! When it comes to bird berry thieves, I've already mentioned the worst offenders: robins, towhees and goldfinches. Around May, robins start hovering near the strawberry beds, which is a great reminder to get the nets up before any red shows on the berries. Robins and blue jays like to chomp on apples—actually, they'll slash big divots into the fruit with their beaks and it quickly spoils. So it helps to have an ample enough crop for you and them both.

**Voles:** As I mentioned numerous times before, vole pressure can be intense. You very seldom see voles, but they do immense damage eating roots and root crops. Since we didn't plant our rhubarb in raised screened beds, the voles killed one of our crowns outright. After losing at least a dozen asparagus crowns to voles, this year, we installed new crowns in screened beds.

Some years back, we turned to technology to combat the voles: we bought six solar-powered stakes that you stick into the ground and emit a very annoying tone every few seconds. The tone had no discernable effect on the voles but drove me crazy! The real bummer was that we'd spent $120 on those stakes. I have used black plastic mulch around the garden to encourage garter snakes to move in (to eat the voles) with some success. But as I already mentioned, you pay a price with plastic. I'll try rock beds next.

My best success with fighting rodents has occurred this spring: I made a concerted effort to dig and clear weedy, wild areas in the yard, particularly adjacent to our strawberry beds. It's been a lot of work, but these spots are where mice and voles just love to hide and hang out until they can sneak under the nets. Since doing all this weeding, I haven't seen one mouse or vole near the strawberries!

The best example of working with nature I've ever seen was in the terrific documentary, **"The Biggest Little Farm."** The film vividly illustrated how a wide range of wildlife keeps pests in check on a sustainable farm. Ladybugs eat aphids; spiders and wasps eat caterpillars; ducks eat snails; snakes and owls eat gophers; and hawks eat starlings. A wonderful balance!

# HOMESTEAD GARDEN CALENDAR

◈

*I*'ve created next section to provide you with an approximate planting and harvesting timeline, to help you schedule your gardening activities. You can make notes on your regular calendar; still, the goal here is to give you a general idea of the important gardening activities month-to-month, and the flow of your garden production throughout the year.

Again, keep in mind that the timeline here is most applicable for the maritime Pacific Northwest. Depending on the growing zone you live in, your local weather conditions and the location of your garden, you can adjust your timeline as needed. A good starting point is to track your first and last average frost dates.

Here are our area's frost dates according to the National Oceanic and Atmospheric Administration (NOAA). First frost: generally between Oct.11-Oct. 20 and last frost: between May 11-May 20.

Here at Berryridge Farm, we'll experience some night temperatures dipping into the 30s as early as mid-August, but no frost. We almost always see the first light frost early in October, around the 4th. You can check your city or county's frost dates at NOAA.gov.

Keep in mind is your gardening calendar will change every year. Temperature and moisture will affect your planting times, germination times, and how fast a crop will ripen or mature.

For example, the last few growing seasons at our place were quite different: a few years ago was a super-long growing season, one of the longest I've experienced. The summer warmth arrived mid-June, and then we had a hot August and warm, dry September.

The following year brought a warm May, a very chilly June, yet a hot August, and a cool and wet September. The year after that, we had a freakishly warm March and a very cold, wet April, with actual snow on April 27th. The summer warmth arrived on time, but August and September was cool and showery.

Your best move is to become a keen observer of weather, moisture, growing patterns, etc. If you have time, keeping a garden journal of your planting, harvesting, and yields will kick your food-raising up a notch or three. Or take photos! We kept a journal for the first five years of homesteading, and it proved to be highly useful.

Since I mention some important information here that the book covered in previous chapters, this timeline can also serve as a "quick-start" guide to starting off your homestead-style garden!

Let's begin with **early Spring gardening:**

**March into April:** At our place, it's far too chilly to plant much of anything in our garden, except perennial crops like berries and new asparagus crowns that can use this cool weather for root development. Likewise, it's too early to sow seeds. I focus on weeding any beds with bare soil, and top dress with compost.

If you have fruit trees, prune them if you didn't get to it in

February. If you need advice and specific techniques, many nurseries and gardening organizations offer pruning classes. Plan the locations of your spring/summer veggie crop beds. Now, to keep your momentum going as the action picks up:

**April:** Weed explosion! Prune blueberries bushes when flower buds swell; plant spinach starts or seeds in ground; sow peas. If you have towhees in your yard, net your pea beds, as towhees will pluck newly germinated peas out of the ground.

End of April, watch for first tips of **asparagus**! When the stalks are 6-8 inches high, time to start harvesting. Cut about 2 inches below the soil line, and wield your knife on a downward slant to avoid damaging neighboring stalks.

**May:** soil is getting warm enough to plant seeds! Foothills average last frost date, May 15. You can sow root crop seeds 2 weeks before the last frost: Carrots, beets, parsnips, seed potatoes.

Potatoes need 50 degrees soil temp for planting. While I haven't taken any soil temperatures, April at our place has proven to be too early for spud-planting—the seed potato might sprout but the plants don't thrive.

Rhubarb: 1st harvest happens right around Mother's Day in the Foothills. Pull gently at base of stalk, easing white portion of plant away from crown. Try not to break stalk at the base.

Asparagus starts serious production in May, so try to pick every day. On warm days, asparagus will grow several inches, and if it gets too tall it may become too woody to eat. The harvest timeframe lasts about six to eight weeks; when the stalks become thin, like pencil-sized, let them keep growing. They'll develop into tall ferns, which helps root development for next year's crop.

**Summer:**

**June: Thin Apples**: remove excess fruits to 1 or 2 per fruit spur. If heavy fruit set, thin to 1 fruit per 5" of branch. Keep weeding your beds.

**Transplant Tomato starts** during a warm spell...for the Foothills, I wait until early June.

**Squash:** Like tomatoes, I'll wait for a warm spell before planting seeds. Chose a plot that gets some heat too!

**June** is strawberry month! Spring temps will determine when the berries are ripe enough to start picking, and once the harvest begins, they'll ripen faster during warm spells. You get about 3 weeks of harvest for June-bearing varieties. Ever-bearing varieties (which bear most of the summer) are nice but I find they're not as high quality berries.

Make sure you sow any root crops you didn't get around to in May; harvest peas regularly for best production. If you let peas mature, the plant thinks it's time to go into seed production, peas get tough and plant goes downhill.

If you're raising hard-neck **garlic**, "scapes" or flower buds will begin to develop on a stalk just as the bulbs are starting to finally put on some size. Make sure you cut off those stalks—they're easy to spot because they have a slightly swollen pointy end! If the scapes are left to develop, the plant will put energy into developing flowers and seeds rather than the garlic bulb.

**Keep in mind:** as late spring/early summer rains end, your food crops need about 1 inch of water/week.

**July:** cane berries start to bear! Mid-month: plant 2nd carrot crop. Peas go downhill with warmer weather. To save pea seeds, let the pods mature on vines until pods are dry and papery. Pea seed-saving doesn't work at our place, since chipmunks and mice tear into the pods. However, I save dried vines for the compost pile!

**Spinach** goes to seed. They develop a tall spike, and leaves lose their sweetness. If you let the stalks continue to develop, as the plants die back, they'll re-seed the bed!

**Later in July: Garlic:** Watch for garlic foliage to die back; when you have 5 dried-up leaves, time to harvest! If you wait too long, the cloves start to separate from head, moisture gets in between the cloves and they'll rot in storage. I keep garlic in our carport (a spot with covered ventilation) until the foliage is totally dry. Then I clip the foliage about an inch from the head, and bring the crop indoors, to store in a cool spot.

**August:** Big harvest month! New potatoes are ready when plants blossom; pick early carrots, more cane berries; blueberries (if you have lots of varieties, your harvest can last 5 weeks or more); cherry tomatoes, summer apples; beets; kale.

**August into September:** Onions: Dry onions in shady, well-ventilated spot before storage. Cut out spent canes on cane berries. Plant seeds/starts for winter crops, like greens; in a mild winter, spinach will winter over and provide early spring crop, also kale and Swiss chard can overwinter.

**Keep watering berry plants after bearing**; plants are developing flower structures for next season. Consider: **Cover crops.** These are crops you plant in fall to protect and build your soil, then the following spring you till them in.

Since we have raised, screened beds you can't really till, we haven't done cover crops. However, later in the summer, I'll plant any extra pea seeds I have on hand. The pea plants don't have time to put on much growth, but the young plants can help "feed" the soil before fall freezes.

**Fall:**

**Late September:** Cranberries are ready to harvest; Delicata squash are ripening too.

**Early to mid- October:** The first frost isn't far away! Before average night temps drop to low 30s, pick the last of your warm-crop stragglers, **zucchini, cucumbers, tomatoes**. (Before the frost turns them into yucky mush.)

**Late Tomatoes:** any green fruits with a hint of yellow may ripen indoors: you can wrap them in newspaper and store in dark location. Tip: wrapping each tomato separately can help prevent blight spoilage.

**Apples**: Mid- to late-season varieties should be harvested, go in fridge. My husband John says apples are best stored in applesauce!

Keep in mind that a homestead-style garden can sometimes provide far more food than you need! Just a few trees, when they mature, can produce a monster harvest.

A few years ago, we harvested thousands of apples from our 12 trees. We packed sacks and sacks of them into both our refrigerators but there were thousands more to deal with. After discovering a local cider-making outfit was seeking local apples, we ended up donating all the extra fruit to the cidery and to my sister for her three horses. We found joy in seeing all that extra harvest getting used, *and* supporting our community!

**Winter squash must** be harvested before the frost hits. For storage, "season" the squash by keeping them in the warmest spot in your house for 10 days, then store in cool, dark spot. **Saving pumpkin seeds?** Dry well, but don't store the seeds in a paper bag in your garage! (We have found piles of squash seeds in our workboots, courtesy of the mice.)

**Root crops**: If you've been selectively harvesting your root crops as they're ready, great! With light frost, allowing your beets to stay in the ground is okay; I finish picking as the weather turns colder. Carrots and parsnips are perfectly fine if you pick as needed; with a touch of frost they get sweeter.

I generally harvest all my carrots by late October, before the beds get too soggy. Parsnips overwinter beautifully through about January. If you leave them in the ground too long, the roots start pushing out new leaves, and the root becomes woody.

**Potatoes**: I've experienced a significant variation in harvest times, depending on summer temperatures. Rule of thumb: watch for the tops to die down, then wait 2 weeks before harvesting. Leaving the potatoes in the soil for that 2 week-period will help toughen the skin. Don't leave them too long, however, since pests start moving in, and you'll find the surface of your spuds have been drilled with little tracks and holes.

This last season, I left my potatoes in the ground well into October; we received so much rain the soil was too wet to dig in for harvesting. Then the Foothills were hit by an early Northeaster: temps in the low 20s. The potatoes growing close to the surface ended up with a lot of frost damage. I ended up losing at least 25% of my crop—but it was a helpful lesson. From here on out, I have vowed to harvest all my spuds on time, well before the possibility of frigid weather!

**Storage:** In past years, I've always rinsed the soil off my spuds, let dry, and stored them in the refrigerator. This past fall, I simply brushed off the excess soil before putting the potatoes in the fridge. These potatoes had to be scrubbed at cooking time, but they kept equally well.

Best practices: you can prepare your potatoes for long-term storage by keeping them in a dark, warmish spot for a couple of weeks, then store in a root cellar. A fridge isn't optimal for potato storage, since the cold will turn the starches into sugars, but it works for John and me.

I've heard of some city gardeners storing potatoes under their house, but in the country, there can be too many pests for "unsecured" storage. Voles would have a party!

**Cane berries: Tie up** the new canes for next year's crop before fall winds hit. Otherwise, the unsecured canes will blow around, and potentially damage neighboring canes, particularly on thorny canes like marionberry.

**Buy seed garlic:** I buy local organic garlic bulbs at the Co-op, or you can buy organic bulbs by mail order or at nurseries. Author Barbara Kingsolver emphasizes that "grocery store" garlic is not suitable for planting—it's been in storage far too long. She also says it has "the shelf life of mummies!"

**Winter greens**: By later October, it's probably too late for seed-sowing; the soil is too cool for germination. You can try plant starts, but mulch well.

**Before serious fall rains:** Add compost for top dressing around caneberry crowns, a little more sawdust or wood chip mulch for blueberry shrubs can't hurt. Asparagus loves a generous application of fall compost.

**Fall to Winter activities for best success the following spring!**

Once veggie beds have been harvested, give them another thorough weeding. Then if your soil warrants it, a sprinkle of dolomite lime; apply mulch, then put compost on top to weigh the mulch down! The compost will add nutrition to soil for next season and helps prevent soil "heaving" (from repeated freeze and thaw cycles). Plus it suppresses weeds in Spring.

I'll emphasize too, that the more preparation you do in fall, with weeding and mulching before tucking your beds in for the winter, the easier and more enjoyable your gardening activities will be by planting time!

**November:** Plant garlic by Thanksgiving! Install pointy head up, "rough, callused" side down. Mulch heavily after planting—I use chopped leaves and lots of compost on top.

You might want to check with a local nursery for timing: One year, we bought seed garlic from an East coast seed outfit, and followed their directions to plant in late September/October. The tops came up before the first winter storm and the whole crop died. I have planted a second bed of garlic in March with mixed results. Protect the spring shoots if you have rabbits.

**More Cool Season/Winter Activities:** Transplanting or new plantings. Give pollinator-friendly perennials a head start for spring! Keep turning your compose pile; turning will help the pile avoid freezing even during cold spells.

**January:** Prune asparagus foliage when it's completely died back.

**Fall and Winter: To create new beds** on lawn or weedy

areas: apply cardboard or newspaper "mulch," cover with heavier material (wood scraps, wood chips, rocks, etc.) so paper or cardboard won't blow away during winter windstorms! If you start a bed in the fall, it's ready by spring!

**Throughout winter:** If you have a fridge in an unheated shop, as we do, check the fridge temp for stored veggies: we keep apples, carrots, and potatoes in our shop fridge. But watch your fridge during cold spells/Northeasters! When outdoor temps hit the low 20s or below, your produce will freeze inside the fridge.

**February:** If the ground isn't frozen, harvest the rest of your parsnips before you see any green tops. Order or purchase your strawberry starts. Seed catalogs are filling your mailbox, so it's easy to research fruit/veggie varieties for spring planting. March is just around the corner and the fun begins again!

# EPILOGUE: LIVING SIMPLY

*Simplifying* your life might sound like doing without life's usual pleasures, but those changes don't have to completely feel like deprivation... Living simply can be a joy, and one way to pursue simplicity is through food choices.

Just between you and me, John and I enjoy imported food like sugar, chocolate, coffee, tea, olive oil, and spices (pretty much) guilt-free. But we've really embraced buying from local growers or food producers whenever possible. Fortunately, our community has all kinds of locally grown products freely available: meat, produce, flour, and even organic chicken feed.

We also focus on buying what's in season and non-GMO food items. Author Barbara Kingsolver shares a revealing story in her memoir *Animal, Vegetable, Miracle*. Some county extension agents tracked raccoons that had discovered two separate stores of corn kernels. One pile was conventional , GMO corn, the other was non-GMO. Guess what? The raccoons didn't touch the GMO corn!

John and I have a pretty modest income and lifestyle, but even if the local, organic, and/or non-GMO foods we enjoy cost a little more, we are happy to pay the higher amount. To me, it's a small price to pay for a healthier world for our eight grand-children to grow up in!

Eating regionally may actually contribute to physical health. Some folks might feel this is a stretch, but a number of health experts say it's better to eat from your local and /or regional "food web"—the soil microorganisms and the crops' biorhythms are more in tune with your body. For example, consider local honey—I've heard eating honey produced near where you live can help allergies!

What's especially important for John and me, however, is that eating locally supports the local economy: in buying area-grown seeds, plant starts and produce, you're supporting the foodways and farmers right in your own community.

Here's another tasty benefit: when you wait to eat a certain food until it's in season, the produce has reached peak flavor and nutrition, and you can look forward to it all the rest of the year! I don't purchase any fresh berries or tomatoes at the grocery store, so that first taste of a homegrown ripe berry or tomato feels like a gift.

When times are uncertain, I have the feeling that nature's gifts are one of the few things we can count on. In the coming season and into the future, I plan to double-down on planting more crops to share. To me, living simply is finding pleasure in little things: good health, an abundant harvest, a meal that came from the garden, and being with my dear ones.

My wish for you is that you and the people you care about stay well, and that today, this week, or this month you can take your first steps toward creating your own thriving food garden... And may your gardening plans and dreams come true!

# AUTHOR'S NOTE

~~~

*A*s I began this book on St. Patrick's Day 2020, in the early days of the corona virus pandemic, your life and mine, and the lives of everyone we know had been turned upside down. Each week brought dire news: cases and deaths skyrocketing, schools and businesses closing, social distancing and quarantines were required, and events, large and small, were cancelled. With the U. S. economy on shaky ground, many folks feared for their jobs and livelihoods. Or experienced the terrible hardships of food insecurity and no longer being able to pay for the roof over their head.

Everyday pleasures all of us took for granted were no longer safe: visiting friends and family, taking part in community activities and attending worship services, or going to a restaurant or the movies.

We withdrew into our homes, growing more panicked and fearful. And if that's not distressing enough, we started to see shortages of basic groceries like flour, meat and toilet paper. Perhaps the most frightening aspect of this global health crisis— apart from the anxiety about our health and that of our dear ones—was discovering that widespread food shortages were actually possible. Our safety and our physical, mental and spiritual wellbeing seemed to be spiraling out of control.

Since those first difficult and frightening days of the pandemic, there's no denying life has changed drastically: whether it was wearing masks, social distancing, or not seeing family or friends. Those deprivations added up, compounding all the challenges we faced in our community, our country and around the world.

Exactly one year later, I updated this section as the corona vaccine became more widely available. As millions of people have been vaccinated, there's hope for the future. The grocery shortages that seemed so scary at the start of the crisis have stabilized; toilet paper is readily available, and little things that you never knew could be so important—like yeast—are back on the store shelves. Still, the economy is not out of the woods, and it will be months before the vaccine is available to everyone.

Yet to me, there's a ray of hope amidst the hardships and tragedies—one positive action that you and I and everyone else can do to cope with this terrible, unforeseen situation: Grow some of your own food. In "normal," everyday life, homegrown food is a pleasure to eat—plus food gardening is a creative endeavor that brings you joy, gets you outdoors, and helps to take your mind off your worries. In these still-uncertain times, it may be that raising some food may become a necessity.

I could never have known, when I planted garlic three months before the pandemic began, that by early spring John and I might have to depend on our garlic crop and the other food we raise in ways we never had before. And as the crisis grew, I got to thinking: what if John and I, like most food growers in our type of climate, were forced to rely on the food we currently had in our garden?

Well, we would go hungry.

Early spring was traditionally known as the "hungry season." As the pandemic kicked in, at our place we had about a dozen parsnips in one bed, and a few overwintered spinach leaves in another, two onions left in the pantry and two dozen garlic heads from last July's harvest. In our freezer, we had four gallons of blueberries, and several quarts of rhubarb. With these items, I guess we could make a big pot of parsnip soup, and have enough breakfast fruit for a few weeks, but clearly, these odds and ends wouldn't last for long.

In summertime, our homegrown food is more bountiful. Although our spring crops are nearly played out by the end of June—like rhubarb, asparagus and spinach—summer's bounty is on the way. By early summer, John and I will be in the middle of strawberry season, looking forward to cane berries, and the peas are in bloom. Still, not many people will thrive for long, eating only a few fruits and vegetables!

It's true, that if you do put in a garden in spring and summer, your crops won't feed you for many weeks or even months. Still, as we find our way out of the pandemic, planting a small food garden, or even trying to grow as much food as possible, may be what restores our health and safety. Not only that, but raising enough food to share with friends, family and neighbors may be what saves our sense of community.

It feels far too soon to think about what our communities and our world will be like after the pandemic. And we may all wonder, will the corona virus always be around?

Yet whatever happens, perhaps more folks might continue living more simply—even in small actions like eating more home-cooked food, doing fewer errands or taking vacations closer to home. Maybe you, like me, have come to more fully appreciate the simple joys in everyday life, like reading a good book, spending more time in nature, and most importantly, enjoying the company of your friends, family, and neighbors.

Whatever your future holds, I hope it includes a garden!

# LITTLE FARM IN THE FOOTHILLS: A BOOMER COUPLE'S SEARCH FOR THE SLOW LIFE

※

*H*ere's Chapter 1 of Susan's first homesteading memoir, *Little Farm in the Foothills: A Boomer Couple's Search for the Slow Life*. Like *Little Farm Homegrown*, the second book of the Little Farm series, Book 1 is a warmhearted, true-life story for gardeners, nature-lovers, and dreamers of all ages!

## 1 * SEEKING WALDEN

It's said that if you want to figure out your life's passion, look at what you loved as a child. When I was growing up, I loved Barbies. You might think, there's a girl who'll go far, what with Astronaut Barbie and Internist Barbie and Professional Figure Skater Barbie. Actually, I predate all those ambitious, take-the-world-by-the-horns Barbies. In *my* time, back in the sixties, all Barbie did was sit around and look hot and wait for Ken to ask her out.

But I also loved to read, especially fairy tales like Sleeping Beauty, and stories about gutsy, courageous girls like Jo March and Laura Ingalls. And when I wasn't reading or hanging out with Barbie, Midge, and Skipper, I was playing in the woods behind our house. Maybe I was living out fantasies inspired by Sleeping Beauty's forest hideaway, or Laura's "Little House" series, but I found my bliss climbing trees, building forts and riding my bike around Woodland Hills, a new development perched on the rural edge of St. Cloud, Minnesota.

My husband, John, was an outdoorsy kid too, with a childhood a lot like mine. (Minus the Barbies.) Your mother sent you outside to play after breakfast, and except for lunch, you were supposed to stay there until it got dark or dinnertime, whichever came first. But then, you didn't really want to be indoors anyway. Certainly not John—from what I can tell, he *lived* "The Dangerous Book for Boys." He'd roam nearby woods and fields with his little gang of friends, playing Robin Hood or cowboys and Indians, coming home so dirty his mom would have to hose him down.

Later, as a young husband and father, John got his fresh air nurturing a small vegetable plot for his family. But it could be the outdoor activities so many of us love as adults, like camping, hiking, and gardening—and I hear vacations on working farms are getting popular!—are a way to free our inner tree-climbing, mud-lovin' child. To return to a simpler time, when most people lived on farms—or at least *knew* a farmer. A time when you spent far more of your life outside than in.

Whatever it is, I never stopped loving the outdoors, and John never lost his longing for wide open spaces...a love and longing we indulged with our mutual passion for gardening. But there came a time when we both yearned for a deeper connection with the land...for a more peaceful life, one more attuned to nature's pace. Okay, that sounds pretty highfalutin'—all we *thought* we wanted was more room for a kitchen garden, and a little quiet in which to enjoy it. Regardless of our goal, our journey to that life began the day we reached our tipping point with urban noise and traffic and crowds...when John and I bucked our play-it-safe, risk-averse natures and decided to leave the city. *Little Farm in the Foothills* is the tale of our fifty-something leap of faith, to seek out a slower, simpler, and more serene lifestyle on a rural acreage. And embrace a whole new way of living.

Who'd have guessed how complicated "simplicity" could get. Or that serenity and reinventing your life was no match made in heaven.

BEFORE I HIT my Boomer years, I'd never seriously considered living in the country.

Despite my woods-playing, I hadn't spent much time in the true boondocks. In elementary school, I'd been a Campfire Girl, but my group never went camping or sat around a campfire—much less lit one. I'd gone tent camping exactly once in my life, a post-high school girlfriend getaway memorable only for the fact that for the entire three days, we'd frozen our eighteen-year-old tushies off. In June!

Anyhow, I'm all for city comforts. Call me picky (I'm the first to admit I'm annoyingly germ-conscious), but I'd always been sort of revolted by the idea of an on-site septic system. There's all that "stuff" in a tank right next to your house, for Pete's sake. And I liked city water. The only well water I'd tasted was loaded with sulfurous compounds, and the rotten-egg smell wafting up from your glass would set off a gag reflex. I didn't want water from just *anywhere*—it could be unhygienic, okay? I have a B.S. in environmental studies. I *know* about contaminated ground-water. I wanted my drinking water from nice clean municipal water treatment plants.

But water was only a side issue. In my youth, I'd had the kind of country experience that would turn most people off permanently...

. . .

*PRAISE FOR LITTLE Farm in the Foothills:*

"The Browne's foray into slower living...is an enjoyable read. Their delightful, yet very real, experiences in making the big leap toward their dreams make for a humorous and charming book." —Washington State Librarian Jan Walsh

"A delightful account." —*The Bellingham Herald*

LITTLE FARM **in the Foothills** is available for free at your local library; you can request the print or ebook version. You can also order a print copy at your neighborhood bookstore, or find the ebook at your favorite online retailer!

# THANK YOU FROM SUSAN

*Dear Reader,*

*Thanks so much for your interest in* Little Farm in the Garden. *I'm always grateful for questions and comments from readers about my books, as well as insights about food-growing, home-steading, or the backyard farming life!*

*Also, if you enjoyed this book, I hope you'll share it with your friends and family.*

*If you have any of your own garden tips, tricks and wisdom to share, I hope you'll get in touch! With your permission, I can share your tips, with credit, on my blog—we'll both be helping other gardens and gardeners thrive!*

*I'm very grateful for your support, and would love to hear from you! You'll find me at my Susan Colleen Browne website, my Little Farm in the Foothills blog, and you can sign up for my newsletter at Little Farm Writer !*

*Kind regards and happy gardening!*
*Susan Colleen Browne*

# ACKNOWLEDGMENTS

I dedicate this book to my mother Nanette, for filling my Minnesota childhood with the vibrant colors of her zinnias and gladiolas, and for sharing her joy and zest for life with everyone she encounters.

Many thanks to all the wonderful students who've attended my "Grow a Homestead-Style Food Garden" class. I've enjoyed talking to each and every one of you, and have been inspired by your questions, comments and gardening insights!

Besides my mom, boundless hugs go to our wonderful family—especially our children and grandchildren, for all the love, friendship and joy they bring into our lives. And I extend my deepest appreciation to my husband John, for his ideas and artistic eye, and especially his support and encouragement. I feel eternally blessed to have him as my true-blue partner all our years together.

# ABOUT THE AUTHOR AND THE PHOTOGRAPHER

Susan Colleen Browne is a graduate of Huxley College of the Environment, Western Washington University. She's the author of an award-winning memoir, *Little Farm in the Foothills,* the first book of the Little Farm in the Foothills series, and the sequel, *Little Farm Homegrown.*

Susan weaves her love of Ireland and her passion for country living into her Village of Ballydara series, novels and stories of love, friendship and family set in the Irish countryside. Her latest Irish novel is Book 7, **The Fairy Cottage of Ballydara**!

She has also created imaginary stories set in the Pacific Northwest: the Morgan Carey fantasy-adventure series for tweens. A community college instructor, Susan runs a little homestead with her husband John in the Pacific Northwest, USA.

When Susan isn't wrangling chickens or tending vegetable beds, she's working on her next Village of Ballydara book!

A retired police sergeant, John F. Browne graduated from Western Washington University with a bachelor's degree in Fine Arts. John is Berryridge Farm's head photographer, firewood slinger, and sodbuster, as well as all-around handy guy and supportive husband!

You'll find recipes, garden tips and chicken tales from Berryridge Farm at Susan's Little Farm blog and her Little Farm Writer Substack newsletter!

# BOOKS BY SUSAN COLLEEN BROWNE

**Little Farm in the Foothills Series**

*Little Farm in the Foothills: A Boomer Couple's Search for the Slow Life,*
Book 1 (print and ebook)

*Little Farm Homegrown: A Memoir of Food-Growing, Midlife, and Self-Reliance on a Small Homestead,* Book 2 (print and ebook)

*Little Farm in the Garden: A Practical Mini-Guide to Raising Selected Fruits and Vegetables Homestead-Style,* Book 3 (print and ebook)

**The Village of Ballydara Series**

*It Only Takes Once,* Book 1 (print and ebook)

*Mother Love,* Book 2 (print and ebook)

*The Hopeful Romantic,* Book 3 (print and ebook)

*The Galway Girls,* Book 4 (print and ebook)

*The Secret Well,* short story ebook

*The Christmas Visitor,* short story ebook and the sequel to *The Secret Well*

*The Little Irish Gift Shop,* Book 5

*Becoming Emma,* Book 6

*Becoming Emma, Special Edition*

*The Fairy Cottage of Ballydara,* Book 7

**The Morgan Carey Series for Tweens, set in the Pacific Northwest**

*Morgan Carey and The Curse of the Corpse Bride,* Book 1, a lighthearted Halloween and Day of the Dead story (print and ebook)

*Morgan Carey and The Mystery of the Christmas Fairies,* Book 2, a gentle fantasy set in the Foothills (print and ebook)

*The Secret Astoria Scavenger Hunt,* Book 3, a haunted house adventure

(print and ebook)

Susan's books are available for **free** in ebook format at your local library—all you have to do is put in a request, or bring up the Libby library app!

The Little Farm books are available in print format at your local library too. You can also order them from your neighborhood bookstore or find them at your favorite online retailer!

# FOOD GARDENING AND
# BACKYARD FARMING RESOURCES

*ooks:*

Carpenter, Novella. *Farm City: The Education of an Urban Farmer.* Penguin Books, 2010.

Deppe, Carol. *The Resilient Gardener: Food production and Self-Reliance in Uncertain Times.* White River Junction, Vt.: Chelsea Green, 2010.

Kimball, Kirsten. *The Dirty Life: A Memoir of Farming, Food and Love.* New York: Scribner, 2011.

Kingsolver, Barbara, et al. *Animal, Vegetable, Miracle: A Year of Food Life.* New York: HarperCollins, 2007.

Pollan, Michael. *In Defense of Food: An Eater's Manifesto.* New York: Penguin Books, 2008.

Solomon, Steve. *Gardening When it Counts: Growing Food in Hard Times.* Gabriola Island, B.C., Canada: New Society Publishers, 2006.

**ADDITIONAL RESOURCES:**

Mother Earth News Magazine, www.motherearthnews.com

Joel Salatin, owner of Polyface Farms in Virginia and the

author of many books including *You Can Farm* and *Folks, This Ain't Normal*; Mr. Salatin also appears in documentary, "Food, Inc." www.polyfacefarms.com

Uprising Seeds, www.uprisingorganics.com

To connect to area farmers, gardeners, homesteaders, and other food-growers, you can check your state's university agriculture extension programs, your local food co-op, and the farmer's markets in your area.

"The Biggest Little Farm" documentary film, 2018, www.biggestlittlefarmmovie.com